An Introduction to Chess Moves and Tactics Simply Explained

(formerly titled: Chess)

By Leonard Barden

Chess Correspondent, *Guardian,*
Field and *Evening Standard*
British Chess Co-Champion, 1954

DOVER PUBLICATIONS, INC. NEW YORK

This Dover edition, first published in 1964, is an unabridged and unaltered republication of the work first published by W. & G. Foyle Ltd., London, in 1959 under the former title: *Chess*. This edition is published by special arrangement with W. & G. Foyle Ltd.

This edition is for sale in the United States of America and its territories only.

Standard Book Number: 486-21210-6
Library of Congress Catalog Card Number 64-18360

Manufactured in the United States of America
Dover Publications, Inc.
180 Varick Street
New York, N.Y. 10014

Contents

CHESS

LEONARD BARDEN has written an admirable introduction to this fascinating game which claims an ever growing number of followers yearly. The author, who was British Chess Co-Champion in 1954 and runner-up in 1958, takes the learner through the first elementary chapters, with the assistance of numerous examples and clear diagrams, up to the stage where he can sit down and play an opponent on his own. After a number of practice games and with the assistance of the later chapters there is nothing to prevent him becoming a proficient player in his own right.

General Editor : W. A. FOYLE

To

M. E. C.

Chapter One

WHY SHOULD YOU PLAY CHESS?

WHY SHOULD YOU learn to play chess? There must be quite a number of you who buy this book or think of buying it who will be doubtful about taking up the game at all. You may, for instance, have seen newspaper cartoons of chessplayers and concluded from these that anyone who takes up the game must be over seventy or, very occasionally, under ten. The easiest way for me to answer this would be to take you along to any chess inter-club or inter-county match. You'd find that the great majority of the players are in their thirties and forties; quite a few are younger, and perhaps one in ten or twenty are over sixty – just about as many as you'd find in any typical cross-section of people. If you went to one of the big international tournaments, you would find that the players were still younger; for most of the top masters in the world are in their twenties, thirties, or forties. Chess is also played a great deal in schools; for instance, Liverpool this year ran a junior congress with over a thousand entries, and the *Sunday Times* organised a National Schools Championship which attracted 246 teams, each of six a side. And one of the greatest players in the world, Bobby Fischer, champion of the United States, is only sixteen. He's pretty exceptional, however. At the other end of the scale, we have, in this country, Douglas Fawcett, the brother of the explorer who disappeared in Brazil, who still attends chess congresses regularly at the age of 92.

Many people are frightened off chess because they think it's necessary to be specially clever or intelligent to play it. If this is so, there must be millions of intelligent people in the world. In the Soviet Union, chess is the national indoor game. In one pre-war trades union championship, there was an entry of 800,000, and if you go on a long journey in a Russian train, it's odds-on that you will be challenged to a game by your fellow-passengers. The Philippines is another country where chess is a national pastime, with tens of thousands of regular competitors. In this country, there are many thousands of people who play regular tournament and county chess, and hundreds of thousands who have learnt the game through books or through the instruction of friends. In other words, you don't need anything more than average intelligence to become a good chess player. It is true that the chess expert, or master, can perform remarkable feats of calculation, concentration, and memory on the chessboard, but the same thing is true of many other occupations, games, and sports. How many cricketers could emulate Test Match batsmen and stay at the crease all day long? How many footballers can juggle the ball like the Brazilians, how many tennis players smash like Drobny? In fact, the man who gets most enjoyment and satisfaction from chess is usually the amateur, making a blunder and then recovering because his opponent makes a worse one, rather than the master, who can never afford to relax his concentration for very long. The ordinary player can admire the art of the master, and can study the fascinating and complicated manoeuvering which goes on in master chess, but he plays with opponents similar in ability to himself and enjoys his own games most of all.

The most formidable red herring of all about chess is the time which it takes. The most common replies of non-chessplayers who are asked if they play the game are 'I'd never have the patience' or 'It takes too long'. What are the facts? A friendly chess game played at home, in a café, or in a chess club, usually takes about an hour to complete. An increasingly popular form of the game is 'lightning chess' in which the players are allowed ten seconds or some other very short interval for each move. And this is one of the great things about chess; a game can be played just as quickly or just as slowly as you like. Now it's true that in games between masters which take place in international events, the average time per game is around five hours; but it shouldn't be thought that even in this case the opponents sit glued to the board, oblivious of anything from a troupe of striptease dancers to a fire in the tournament hall. If you ever watch a master chess tournament, you'll find that most of the competitors walk around talking to their friends or watching the other games while their opponents are thinking. There are a few masters who sit at the board for the whole of a session, but they are the exception and not the rule.

What about the patience you need for chess? Once you've learnt the game, this isn't a question you'll want to ask any more. For a chess game is crammed full of excitement and interesting problems for the players, so that you become absorbed in the same way as if you were reading a good novel or watching a first-class theatre performance.

Chess is an easy game to learn. The rules, as explained in the first part of this book, will take you, probably, an hour or two to absorb ; and you can then, if you want to, sit down and play your first game of chess straightaway. The next part tells you how you can plan your strategy and set traps which will help you to win your games ; it also explains the special notation used by chess players to record their games. At first sight, these abbreviations look like some obscure code ; but they just represent a simple shorthand method of naming the pieces and the squares of the chessboard. When you understand chess notation, you will be able to play over and enjoy games from master tournaments and championships, as published in newspapers, magazines, and books.

The final part of the book should be of interest to those who already know something about chess, as well as those taking up the game for the first time. It tries to show what sort of general principles to keep in mind during a game, and the ways to improve if you want to become a strong player.

Chapter Two

HOW THE GAME IS PLAYED

To play chess, you need a chessboard and a set of chessmen. Although it's perfectly possible to use a small and inexpensive pocket board, you'll find that if you want to enjoy your games with friends in comfort that it's a good idea to get a full-size set. You should be able to buy one of these from any good department store or games shop. The pieces of a ' Staunton design ' are by far the most popular nowadays, and indeed you should beware of buying expensive sets of other designs which may look beautiful, but are less easily distinguishable during an actual game.

The 64 squares on the board are coloured alternately white and black (on an actual board which you buy, cream and black is the easiest combination on the eyes to have. Other colour schemes, such as red and black, are less advisable). Each player has 16 pieces or ' men '. The photograph shows what they look like in your Staunton-type set.

Fig. 1

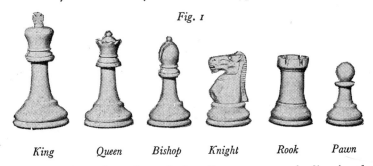

| King | Queen | Bishop | Knight | Rook | Pawn |

The main point of confusion for most people lies in the difference between the king and queen. In almost every type of set, however, the king will have a small cross at the top, and the queen will be slightly smaller and have a ridged edge to the top, like a coronet.

Figure 2 shows the chessboard set up at the beginning of

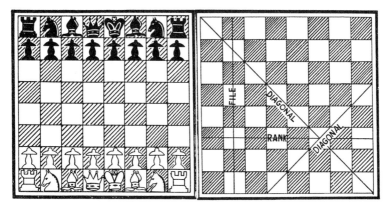

Fig. 2 – The Starting Position.   *Fig. 3 – Files, Ranks, and Diagonals.*

the game. In this illustration, the chessmen are shown by the symbols by which they are represented throughout the book.

Reading from left to right, the pieces in this Figure are rook, knight, bishop, queen, king, bishop, knight, rook. In front of them, is the row of eight pawns. Two points should be specially remembered when you set up the men for the beginning of the game : first, the board is always placed with a *black square in the bottom left-hand corner.* It is surprising how often this is forgotten even by comparatively experienced players. The second thing which often causes confusion is which way round to put the king and queen. If you have the board the right way round, then it's easy ; the *white* queen always goes on a *white* square, the *black* queen on a *black* one.

THE MOVES OF THE CHESSMEN

Before we go on to the actual moves of the pieces, it must be mentioned that chess has its own terminology for the horizontal and vertical lines on the chessboard, as shown in Figure 3.

The Rook.

The rook (occasionally you may hear it called the castle,

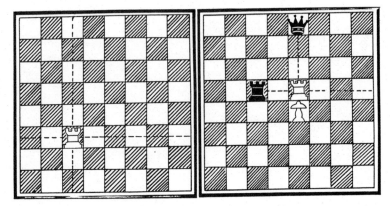

Fig. 4 – How the rook moves.　　　*Fig. 5 – How the rook captures.*

but this name isn't in general use) moves horizontally and
vertically, along the ranks and files. Thus, in Figure 4, the
rook can move to any of the squares along the dotted lines.
Capturing in chess is done, NOT by jumping over the captured
piece (as in draughts) but by taking the captured piece off
the board and substituting the capturing piece on that square.
This can be seen in operation in Figure 5. The white rook
can move along the rank to its right to any of the three squares
as far as the edge of the board, for there is nothing in the way.
Alternatively, it can move one square to its left; or it can
go two squares to the left, remove the black rook from the
board, and instal itself on the vacated square. It can't go
three, four, or five squares to its left because that would mean
jumping over a piece. The rook can also go up or down the
board along the file. It can go one or two squares up the
board to a new square, or go three squares up the board and
capture the black queen. CAPTURES IN CHESS ARE OP-
TIONAL; the rook doesn't HAVE to make a capture when it
can. Can it go down the board? No, for that would mean
removing the white pawn (you can't capture your own piece)
or jumping over it (which again it's not allowed to do).

The Bishop.

A bishop moves diagonally, as in Figure 6; from which you

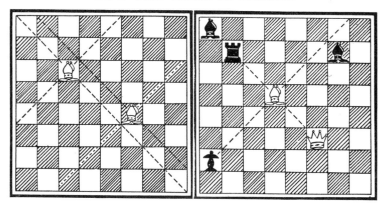

Fig. 6 – How the bishops move.   *Fig. 7 – The bishop may travel any desired number of squares in one move, provided there is nothing in the way.*

will readily see that a bishop which starts off on a white square can never move to a black one, and vice-versa. It captures in the same manner as a rook ; thus in Figure 7, the white bishop can, if it wishes, capture either the black rook or the black pawn ; but it cannot jump over the rook to capture the black bishop in the corner, nor can it jump over its own queen. You have two bishops, and one of them moves only on white squares, the other only on black.

One point which you should note about a bishop is that when it is on the edge of the board it commands substantially fewer squares (seven) than when it is posted in the centre (thirteen).

The Queen.

The queen is the most powerful piece on the chessboard, and when she really gets going she can wreak havoc in the enemy position. As you will see from Figures 8 and 9, the queen combines the moves of the rook and the bishop. Once again, captures with the queen are made by removing the captured piece from the board and substituting the queen on the square concerned.

17

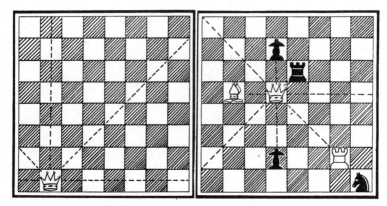

Fig. 8 – How the queen moves.

Fig. 9 – The queen can capture any of the black pieces except the knight in the corner.

The Knight.

The knight is the most alarming piece of all to beginners, for it is the only one that is permitted to jump over other men ; and in consequence (until you get used to it) it often seems to appear in the middle of your pieces from nowhere.

The easiest way to remember the knight's move is in the

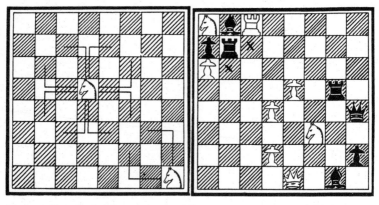

Fig. 10 - How the knight moves ; in the form of a letter L or from one corner to the opposite corner of a 3 x 2 rectangle.

Fig. 11 – How the knight captures and leaps over other pieces.

form of a capital L ; although the L may be upside down or sideways, as in the two examples in Figure 10. But you can also think of the knight's move as from one corner of a 3 × 2 rectangle to the opposite one. Note that a knight always moves from a black square to a white square, or vice versa.

In Figure 11 there is illustrated the knight's ability to jump over intervening pieces. Although the knight in the corner square is surrounded by both its own and enemy pieces, it can still move to either of the squares marked x, just as if those pieces were not on the board. When capturing, the knight follows the normal process of removing the captured piece and substituting itself. In the bottom right-hand corner of Figure 11, the knight can capture any of the four black men, but cannot move to any of the four squares occupied by its own men. Figure 12 shows how a knight can jump over either its own or its opponent's men to effect a capture ; in the top position, it captures the black queen, in the bottom the black rook.

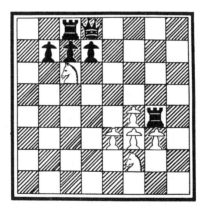

Fig. 12 – The knight jumps over other pieces when it wants to make a capture.

The knight, even more than the bishop or the queen, is handicapped when placed in a corner square rather than a central one. In Figure 10, the knight in the centre has eight squares available, the one in the corner a mere two.

The Pawn.

Fig. 13

The pawn, the foot soldier of the chessboard, has one characteristic which any army commander would heartily approve of : it can only move forwards, and NEVER backwards. Normally, the pawn moves forward one square at a time, but on its first move it has the option, if desired, of moving forward two squares. You can see this in Figure 13A. (Incidentally, in this and all other illustrations in this book, White is assumed to be playing UP the board, Black DOWN. To save space, four separate positions are given on this one diagram, but in each case the whole board is taken to be included). The left-hand pawn in Figure 13A, on its initial square, has the option of advancing one square or two. The other pawn, however, cannot move at all ; for it is blocked by the rook (only knights can jump over other pieces).

In Figure 13B, the left-hand pawn can simply move forward one square. The other pawn, which has advanced nearly the whole length of the board, illustrates one of the most important characteristics of a pawn. For when it completely crosses the board and reaches the eighth line or rank, it is exchanged for any other piece, barring the king. Normally, such a pawn is promoted to the all-powerful queen, and this is why the advantage of a pawn in the later stages of a game is often decisive. The exchange of the pawn at the eighth rank for a piece counts as part of the move. Incidentally, if you have a case such as that of Figure 13B, and you want to make the pawn into a queen, you can use a rook upside down or a coin to symbolise the promotion if the original queen is still on the board.

Figure 13C shows how a pawn captures. Like all the other pieces, it does so by substituting itself on the square of the captured piece, which is simultaneously removed from the board ; but whereas the pawn advances forwards, it captures one square diagonally forward. You cannot move your pawn forward diagonally unless it is capturing an enemy man ; and it cannot move straight forward if the road is blocked by something else. In Figure 13C, the left-hand pawn has the option of advancing one square, advancing two, or of capturing the black bishop. The right-hand pawn has a similar choice, but the centre pawn cannot move at all. It cannot move directly forwards because the bishop is in the way ; and it cannot move diagonally forwards because there is nothing to capture.

The rear left-hand white pawn in Figure 13D cannot move forwards, since it is blocked by its own pawn (it would make no difference if it was an enemy pawn), but it can capture the black pawn one square diagonally forward. The right-hand white pawn has a pleasant choice ; it can advance directly forward and become a queen or any other piece except the king ; or, alternatively, it can capture either the bishop or the rook, again simultaneously becoming a piece.

No restriction is placed upon the number of pawn-promotions, so that it is theoretically possible to have nine queens at once. Normally, however, there are not more than one or two promotions during a game.

Figure 14 shows a situation at White's end of the board. The white pawn in Figure 14A is on his second rank, at the original square. If White advances his pawn forward one square, then Black can capture it with his own pawn by moving one square diagonally forward. If White instead moves his pawn two squares forward, there is a special rule

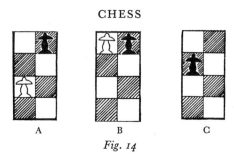

A B C

Fig. 14

known as the *en passant* rule, according to which Black can,
if desired, take off the pawn just as if it had only moved one
square. This option can only be exercised at the very
moment when the pawn is advanced two squares and cannot
be postponed until later in the game. So in Figure 14A we
see the situation before White has advanced his pawn two
squares, Figure 14B shows the situation immediately after this
move, and Figure 14C shows Black having captured the pawn
just as if it had only advanced one square. Remember that
the pawn only has the option of advancing two squares on
its first move; so that an en passant situation can only arise
when one player's pawn has advanced to the fifth rank and
the other's pawn on the adjacent file is unmoved.

The King.

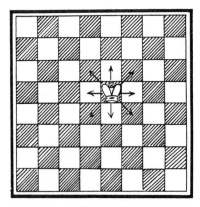

Fig. 15 – How the king moves.

The king is not a particularly strong piece in itself ; it can only move one square at a time, in any direction. But in another, much more important sense, the king is the most vital piece on the whole chessboard ; for the ultimate object of the whole game is to attack your opponent's king and bring about a situation in which its capture is inevitable. Just how this can be done, and what modification this makes to the rules outlined so far, is the subject of the next chapter.

Chapter Three

CHECKS, CHECKMATES, AND STALEMATES

THE OBJECT OF of a game of chess is to checkmate the opposing king. You are not allowed actually to capture a king, but if a situation arises in which this capture is inevitable, the king is said to be ' checkmated ' and the game is over. If the king is attacked by an opposing piece (that is to say, if he is threatened with capture on the next move), he is said to be ' in check '. It is customary to announce ' check ' when you make a move which attacks the king.

The player whose king is threatened MUST make a move which takes away his king from attack. There are three methods of escaping from a check :

(a) By removing the king to another square which is not attacked by an opposing piece.

(b) By capturing the attacking (checking) piece, either with the king or with another piece.

(c) By interposing a man between the king and the attacker.

If none of these resources are available, and there is no way at all for the king to avoid being captured next move, then the king is checkmated.

Since the king may not be in check, it follows that the king may not capture a checking piece which is defended. You cannot, either, have the two kings on adjacent squares ; for then both sides would be in check simultaneously. Remember this ; it is a mistake which beginners often make.

CHECKS

Here are some examples of checks. In Figure 16A, the black king is in check from the bishop. Black has the choice of (a) moving his king to either of the adjacent white squares (he cannot go to the black square because he would still be

Fig. 16 – Checks.

under attack by the bishop). (b) Interposing the pawn in the way of the check. (c) Capturing the bishop with the rook.

In Figure 16B the king is in check from a knight. Interposition is impossible against a knight check ; and so Black has the choice between moving his king or capturing the checking knight with his queen or rook.

In Figure 16C, White can move his knight to any square, and this will reveal check from the queen which is behind the knight. This is known as a ' discovered check '.

In Figure 16D, in a similar situation to 16C, White has been able to move his knight away and deliver check with this piece as well as with the queen. This is known as a ' double check ' and is one of the most dangerous types of attack, since it is impossible to interpose against both checks simultaneously or capture both checking pieces at once. In the case of a double check, the king *must* move ; and in this example he has only two available squares. Other squares are attacked by the white queen or pawn, or occupied by his own pawn.

CASTLING

Before we go on to checkmates and see how chess games end, there is one special move which must be mentioned.

Fig. 17 – Castling.   A   *Fig. 18*   B

Once during a game a king is allowed to make a joint move with a rook during which they pass over each other. This can be done either on the queen's side or on the king's side. In each case, the king moves two squares towards the rook, and then the rook moves over the king to the square immediately on the other side (see Figures 17 and 18). Figure 18A shows the queen's side castling completed, and 18B the king's side completed. When you castle, you should grasp your king either before or simultaneously with the rook ; if you take hold of the rook first, your opponent can legally compel you to make just a rook move.

Castling is illegal if (a) either the king or the rook concerned has already been moved, or (b) the king is in check, or (c) the king has to cross a square attacked by an enemy piece (it does not matter if the rook is attacked or has to cross an attacked square), or (d) the square on which the king lands is attacked by an enemy piece, or (e) there is another piece, either friendly or opposing, in the path of the manoeuvre.

In Figure 19A, White cannot castle at all, because his king is in check from a bishop. If the bishop is removed from the board, what happens then ? White cannot castle king's side, because the square on which the king would land is attacked by a knight ; but he can castle queen's side, although the rook would have to cross an attacked square. In Figure 19B,

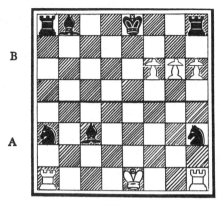

Fig. 19

Black cannot castle queen's side because one of his own pieces is in the way ; but he can castle on the king's side (none of the pawns attack any of the squares across which the king must pass).

Castling is a device which is employed by both sides in the majority of games. The reason is that the safety of the king is paramount, and in the centre of the board the king is more exposed to attack than when he is out of the way on the wing.

Some beginners have a mistaken idea that castling is illegal once the king has been in check. This is wrong : provided that in getting out of check the king was not moved castling is permitted later in the game.

CHECKMATE

Figures 20 and 21 show four examples in each of which the black king is checkmated. In 20A, the four white pieces combine in a mating attack. The white-squared bishop attacks the king, and the other bishop, the knight, and the pawn play their part by guarding various possible escape squares. In 20B, the king is attacked by the white bishop, and the possible escape squares are either occupied by other black pieces or guarded by the white rook. Note particularly in this example that the attacking bishop cannot be captured, either by the king (which would then be in check from the guarding rook) or

27

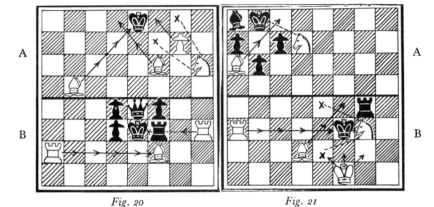

Fig. 20   *Fig. 21*

by the black rook (since the king would then be left in check from the other white rook).

In 21A, we see a checkmate by a knight; the escape squares are guarded by the white bishop or occupied by black pieces. In 21B, various white pieces combine in the attack. Note particularly that the king cannot go on to a square next to the white king; nor can the white knight be captured, since the king would still be in check from the rook.

STALEMATE

From time to time a position arises (normally when only a few pieces are left on the board) in which one side, while not being in check, has no legal move either with the king or with any of the other pieces, although it is that player's turn to move. In such a case, the game is counted as a draw, even though the side which has no move may be heavily down in material. He is said to be 'stalemated'.

Figure 22A is a typical situation when a player who is far ahead in material becomes careless; although Black's king is surrounded, he is not in check and is stalemated. If it were White's turn to move, he could checkmate at once in several ways.

In Figure 22B, the king and the pawn between them guard all the squares to which the black king could possibly move; but the black king is not in check, and is therefore stalemated.

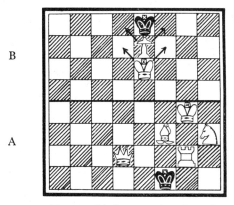

Fig. 22 – Black to move is stalemated.

Were it White's turn to move, he could move his king and this would in turn allow Black to make a move. Such a situation is important in practical play; for there are a number of endgames (an endgame is the phase of the game when few pieces are left on the board) in which a position like that of the position in 22B can be aimed for by the weaker side as a means of drawing the game.

OTHER WAYS OF ENDING A GAME

Besides checkmate and stalemate, a game can end in the following ways :

(1) By resignation. When a player is hopelessly behind in material against an opponent of equal or similar strength, or sees that checkmate is inevitable in a few moves, he often resigns the game rather than continue a hopeless resistance. If you are a complete beginner, however, you should not resign – you will learn more by seeing how the actual check-mating process is carried out, and if your opponent is also a beginner it is quite possible that he will make a terrible blunder and not win at all. As you gain more experience, however, you will recognise that there are positions which are completely hopeless against a reasonably practised opponent ; and in such cases it is better to resign and start a new game

rather than waste his and your own time by prolonging a futile struggle.

(2) Because of inadequate force to checkmate. A lone king can never checkmate a lone king, and there are other endgames, like king and bishop against king or king and knight against king, in which checkmate is equally impossible. If neither side has sufficient material to checkmate, the game is a draw.

(3) By an agreement to draw. In completely even endings, such as in Figure 23, it is customary for the players to agree to a draw, since only a tremendous blunder could permit a win by either side. If there are no pawns to be queened and the remaining material is even, there is rarely any reason for continuing the game.

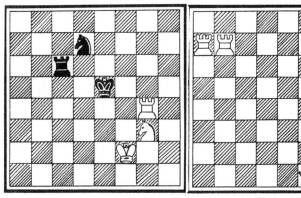

Fig. 23 – In positions like this, the players agree to a draw.

Fig. 24 – Black, to move, gives perpetual check with his queen.

(4) By a draw by perpetual check. In Figure 24, Black is hopelessly behind in material and threatened with checkmate in one move. But he can draw by checking the white king as indicated, whereupon White has only one possible move with his king. Black checks again at the original square, and once again the king has only one move. This process can continue *ad infinitum*, and hence we get the term ' perpetual check '. It is a useful resource which is quite often a saving clause in a lost position.

(5) By a draw by repetition of position. If the same position occurs three times with the same player to move each time, then the side whose turn it is to move can claim a draw.

(6) By the 50-move rule. The rules of chess state that you must deliver mate within 50 moves in positions where such a mate can be forced within this number of moves. Otherwise, providing a pawn has not been moved or a capture made during this period, a draw can be claimed.

Cases (5) and (6), particularly the latter, rarely occur outside tournament and match play.

MISCELLANEOUS TERMS AND RULES

' En Prise '. To place a piece ' en prise ' means to put it where it can be captured.

Fork. A fork is an attack on two pieces on the same time. Beginners have the most occasion to fear forks, for if you are not yet well acquainted with the powers and moves of the pieces, you will often find one of your opponent's pieces simultaneously attacking two of yours. The most common type of fork is that of Figure 25A, in which the white knight simultaneously gives check and attacks the black queen. Since priority must be given to getting out of check, the powerful queen is lost in exchange for the knight.

Other pieces, however, can give forks. In 25B, the white pawn is attacking both rooks, one of which must be lost.

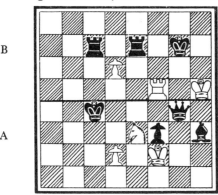

Fig. 25

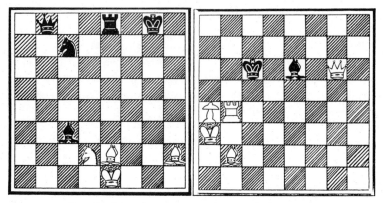

Fig. 26 – Pins.

Fig. 27 – The white king cannot move,
although the black bishop is pinned.

Pin. In Figure 26, neither the white knight nor the bishop on the white square can legally move, because to do so would expose the white king to check from the black rook or bishop ; these pieces are said to be ' pinned '. The black knight can legally move ; but if it does so, the powerful black queen can be captured by the white bishop on the black square. A pin, therefore, also includes situations where to move a piece would expose a more important one to capture.

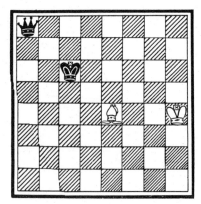

Fig. 28 – Skewer.

A pinned piece can still give check. In Figure 27, the white king cannot move to either of the adjoining white squares, even though the checking piece, the bishop, is completely pinned against the black king and unable to move at all.

Skewer. This term is not in such common use as the fork and pin, but it provides an apt description of such positions as Figure 28. Black's king is in check, and must therefore expose the queen behind it to capture. The king and queen are ' skewered ' like pieces of meat in a butcher's shop.

Fianchetto. A fianchetto is when the bishop is developed on the long diagonal by either P – KKt3 or P – QKt3, followed by B – Kt2.

Chapter Four

CHESS NOTATION

ONE ENORMOUS ADVANTAGE which chess has over the great majority of other games is that to get a record of what happened in an important international contest or in your own friendly encounters is quite easy. There is a special notation which enables you to take down in a convenient shorthand form all that has happened. In this book I shall deal with the English notation, which is used in all English-speaking countries; although on the continent a different and, in my opinion, much simpler system, is universally adopted. However, as you will find that all books and newspaper columns in this country use the English notation, it is as well to concentrate on it exclusively.

The fundamental idea of chess notations is that the pieces and the squares on the chessboard are named in abbreviated form. For the pieces, the symbols are :

King	.	.	. K
Queen	.	.	. Q
Rook	.	.	. R
Bishop	.	.	. B
Knight	.	.	. Kt (occasionally N is used)
Pawn	.	.	. P

Every square on the chessboard is given two names, according to whether it is being considered from White or Black's viewpoint. Looked at from White's side, the squares on which the pieces stand at the beginning of the game are named from them. Thus, the square on which the queen stands is Q1, and the square on which the knight nearest the king stands is KKt1. Reading from left to right along the bottom of the board, the squares are QR1, QKt1, QB1, Q1, K1, KB1, KKt1, and KR1. Each piece gives its name not only to its own starting square but also to all the other squares on that file or column. Thus, the square in front of the king is K2, then comes K3, and so on all the way to K8, which is the square on which Black's king stands at the beginning of the game.

Now one can see why each square has two names. For, from Black's viewpoint, his K1 is the same as White's K8. In Figure 29, every square on the board is numbered twice; the right way up for White and upside down for Black.

BLACK

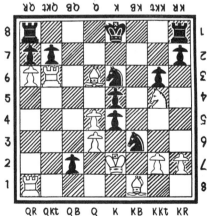

WHITE

Fig. 29 – Chess notation.

Figure 30 shows how chess notation is used in practice.

Fig.. 30 – Chess notation.

Let us assume it is White's move, and he wants to advance his king's knight's pawn (that is, the pawn in front of his king's knight at the start of the game) two squares. He could write down KKtP to KKt4, but this would be unnecessarily cumbersome. Since pawns move directly forward, no other pawn can reach this square, so you can simply write P – KKt4; the dash signifies ' moves to '. But even this can be shortened, for White has no QKtP on the board ; so the move is simply written P – Kt4.

Captures are denoted with an × ; so that if we want to say that the white bishop on Q6 has captured the black pawn on K5, we write B × P (there is no other pawn that either white bishop can capture). What if the white knight wants to capture the black knight on White's K6 ? We cannot simply write Kt × Kt, since the second black knight is also liable to capture. The answer is Kt × Kt(K6). Note here that the capture is reckoned from the side of the *player making the move* ; even when the player of Black is writing down the move, it still remains White who actually plays it.

Now let us consider what to write down if White wants to capture the black pawn on his K5 with his own pawn on Q4. To write simply P × P would be ambiguous, for there are two other white pawns which can capture black pawns. Nor would P × KP be sufficient, for White has two pawns, either of which can capture a black king's pawn. So here it is necessary to write P × P(K5). Note again that we write K5 and not K4, for it is a *White move*, and therefore described from *White's viewpoint*.

Another tricky case occurs if White wants to move his rook from QR1 to QKt1. It is not sufficient to write simply R – Kt1, for the other rook can also move there. So we can write R(R1) – Kt1. It is not necessary to put QR1, because there is no rook on KR1 ; and it is not necessary to specify that this is QKt1, because the rook cannot go to KKt1. Another possibility in such cases, assuming that the rook to be moved is the queen's rook, still on its original square, is to put QR – Kt1 ; but it is best to avoid this unless the move occurs at an early stage of the game when it is quite clear which rook is meant by the queen's rook.

Now let us assume that it is Black's turn to move in Figure 30. He advances his king's rook's pawn one square ; how is it noted down ? Is simply P – R3 sufficient, when another black pawn can go to Black's QR3 by capturing the white pawn on that square ? The answer is yes, for the latter move would be written P × RP (it is necessary to specify the RP because there are two other black pawns which can make pawn captures).

Now suppose that the pawn on Black's K5 takes the pawn on Black's Q6, giving check to the white king. Must we write down P × P(Q6) check ? No, for there is only one pawn that can capture a pawn and simultaneously give check. So, since ch. is the recognised abbreviation for check, we write P × P ch. Now suppose that the black knight on Black's KB6 takes the white pawn on Black's Q5, again giving check to the white king ? To write Kt × P ch is ambiguous, since the other knight can also capture this same pawn, so we must describe it as Kt(B6) × P ch. There is no need to specify which B6, because there is no knight on QB6 ; and there is no need to put QP rather than just P, for there is no other pawn which the knight can capture with check. If the knight on KB6 wants to capture the king's rook's pawn instead, the move need only be written as Kt × P and not Kt × RP, since there is no other pawn that either knight can capture without check.

Castling on the king's side is sometimes written Castles KR and sometimes o – o, while on the queen's side it is described as Castles QR or o – o – o (you can remember this difference easily because in queen's side castling the rook moves three squares towards the king, in king's side castling only two). In Figure 30, however, Black cannot castle on the king's side because the white bishop guards one of the squares which the king must cross ; therefore, if Black castles on the opposite wing in this case, we need only write Castles (or o – o – o).

Other recognised abbreviations are 'mate' instead of checkmate, and P × P e.p. when a pawn is captured en passant. In recorded chess games, the sign ! means a fine, unexpected, or brilliant move, the sign ? a doubtful, in-different, or bad move. Just how strong is the praise or

37

censure in each case clearly depends on the attitude of the person describing the game ; one well-known continental annotator very often puts !!! after his own moves when his games are published in chess magazines.

Here now are the opening moves of a game given in chess notation.

White	*Black*
1. P – Q4	

This means that White's first move is the pawn at the square Q2 to the square Q4. No other pawn can move there.

1. ...	P – Q4

Black's pawn from his Q2 square goes to his Q4.

2. P – QB4	

White's queen's bishop's pawn advances two squares.

2. ...	P × P

The black pawn captures the pawn on Black's QB5. No other pawn capture is possible.

3. Q – R4 ch.	

The white queen comes out to QR4, giving check. It is not necessary to give the full name of this square, since the queen can only go to one of the R4s.

3. ...	P – B3

Black interposes a man between the checking piece and his king. We need only write P – B3 and not P – QB3 because a move with the other bishop's pawn would be illegal ; it would still leave the king in check.

4. Q × BP	

This could equally well be written Q × P(B4). Simply Q × P is not enough, for the queen could also capture the pawn on White's QR7. However, Q × BP can only mean the pawn on White's QB4 and not the one on his QB6, for this would have to be written Q × P ch.

4. ...   Kt – Q2

The knight from Black's QKt1 moves to Q2. It is not necessary to specify which knight as the other knight cannot reach this square.

5. Kt – KB3

White's knight at KKt1 moves to KB3.

5. ...   KKt – B3

This could also be written Kt(Kt1) – B3. It is necessary to specify which knight goes to B3 in this case, for either one can move there ; but since it is very early in the game, it is quite clear that by KKt we mean the knight on KKt1.

6. P – Q5

The pawn on White's queen's fourth moves on one square.

6. ...   P – K4

Black advances his king's pawn two squares.

7. P × P e.p.

White's pawn on the fifth rank has the option of taking ' en passant ' the pawn on the adjacent file which has bypassed it by advancing two squares, and does so. It is unnecessary to specify that it is the king's pawn which has been taken because only one en passant capture is possible in this, and indeed in any position (remember an en passant capture can only be made immediately the pawn has advanced two squares).

7. ...   B – Kt5 ch.

Black moves his bishop out to queen's knight's fifth, giving check.

8. K – Q1

White's king moves from its original square to the one originally occupied by the queen.

8. ...   Kt – K4 dis. ch.

The black knight at Q2 moves to his K4, discovering check from the black queen on to the white king. Note that discovered check is written in this way ; db. ch. stands for double check.

9. QKt – Q2

The white knight at QKt1 moves to Q2. It is necessary to say which knight because the other knight can move there as well.

9. ...   Kt × Q

The black knight captures the white queen.

10. K – B2

The white king moves to QB2.

10. ...   0 – 0

The black king castles with the black rook. We now have the position shown in Figure 31.

Fig. 31 – Position after Black's 10th move. (This is, incidentally, a far from faultless game, since it includes several blunders; but it is included primarily to help you understand chess notation.)

TAKE A REST !

If you have read through the book this far at one sitting without previously knowing anything of chess, you are probably completely bewildered and have only the haziest idea of what a stalemate or a perpetual check are. Don't

worry, for what you should do now is to lay the book aside
completely for the time being and find a friend (preferably a
little beyond the beginner stage) who will play some games
with you. That way you will get the moves of the pieces
firmly fixed in your mind, and also refresh yourself about
checks, checkmate, castling, and so forth. Then you should
come back to this book and re-read these first four chapters.
For further practice, place a dozen or so pieces haphazardly
on the chessboard and move them around, white and black
alternately, capturing, checking, and if possible reaching
checkmate or stalemate positions. Then spend an hour or so
simply recording moves, remembering particularly that they
are to be reckoned from the side of the player making the
move and turning the board round after each move to help
you. Chess notation is particularly worth while spending a
little time on, for once you have grasped it thoroughly you
will be able to start trying to solve chess problems in newspapers and playing over the games of the great masters (even
though, as yet, you will have very little idea of what they are
about).

If you have no one available to play with you at the
moment, then still move the pieces around on the chessboard
and practice taking down the moves before re-reading these
four chapters. By way of extra practice in chess notation and
the moves of the pieces, try answering the following questions
on Figure 31 (see page 40).

1. The black bishop on Black's QB1 captures the white
pawn ; how is this written down ?

2. How many pieces in Figure 31 have no legal move ?

3. If the white king can, in the next two moves, retreat to
K1, can he still castle later on in the game ?

4. The white pawn on KKt2 advances two squares ; how
is this written ?

5. The white pawn on White's K6 takes the black pawn ;
how is this described ?

Solutions.

1. B × P. 2. Three ; the two white bishops and the

white KBP. 3. No. You can never castle if either the
king or the rook concerned have already moved during
the game. 4. P – Kt4 (the QKtP cannot advance two
squares since QKt4 is occupied by the black bishop).
5. P × P ch.

Chapter Five

ELEMENTARY ENDGAMES

THE ENDGAME IN chess is not exactly defined ; but for practical purposes you can call it that part of the game in which the forces are so far reduced that checkmating attacks are no longer likely. With only three or four pieces left on each side, the king can venture forth from his hideout in the rear of the board and become an active fighting force. Pawn promotion replaces checkmate in the endgame as a major objective ; for once you have converted one of your pawns into a queen your superiority in force is likely to be so overwhelming that achieving checkmate becomes relatively easy. For this reason, the advantage of a single pawn in the ending is very often decisive.

However, before studying the strategy of pawn promotion, it is essential to know how to win the game once the pawn has been promoted – which is why this chapter starts off with the ending of king and queen against king.

MATE WITH KING AND QUEEN

The beginner's natural reaction to the position in Figure 32 will be to harass the king with a series of checks, e.g. 1. Q – B5 ch, K – Q5 ; 2. Q – B4 ch, K – Q4 ; 3. Q – B3 ch, K – K4 (the black king stays in the centre) ; 4. Q – K2 ch, K – Q4 and so on – by which time it is clear that we are getting nowhere fast. If you try to construct a position in which the queen alone checkmates the lone king, you will find quickly that it is impossible ; you need the help of the king. Furthermore, a mating position can only be reached at the side of the board. This makes the strategy of this ending clear ; you use the king and queen in combination to drive the king to the side of the board, and there you checkmate him.

1. Q – Q7

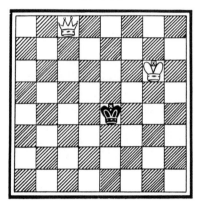

Fig. 32 – Use the king and queen together !

To begin with, the king's movements are restricted.

    1. ...   K – B5

If 1. ..., K – K4 ;   2. K – Kt5, K – K5 ;   3. Q – Q6, and the king is further restricted.

    2. Q – K6   K – B6
    3. K – Kt5

The white king joins in crowding the enemy backwards.

    3. ...   K – Kt6
    4. Q – K2

Now the king must retreat to the edge of the board – the ideal situation for the mating side.

    4. ...   K – R6

Now we come to a situation in which millions of beginners have fallen headlong over the last few hundred years. If White tries to restrict the king still further by 5. Q – B2, then Black has no move, but he is also not in check ; so it is STALEMATE, the game is drawn, and there will be great weeping and gnashing of teeth.

    5. K – B4!   K – R5

Now Black has got a move.

6. Q – R2 mate.

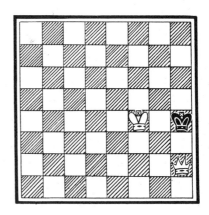

Fig. 33 – Final position; note that the white king stands directly opposite the black king, where it does a lot to stop it escaping.

MATE WITH KING AND ROOK

Quite often in the endgame, one side will have to give up a rook for a pawn to stop the pawn queening, which explains why you should also be sure that you know how to mate with king and rook against king. The principle is the same; use the king and rook in combination, and drive the enemy king to the edge of the board, for it is only there that he can be mated.

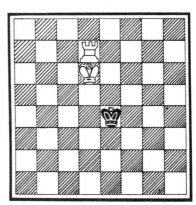

Fig. 34 – King and rook against king.

1. K – B5   K – K4

The king tries to remain in the centre.

2. R – K7 ch

Compare this position with Figure 33 ; once again the direct opposition of the two kings is a great help in driving the weaker side back.

2. ...	K – B5
3. K – Q5	K – B6
4. R – K4	

The black king is now confined to a small part of the board.

4. ...	K – Kt6
5. K – Q4	K – B6
6. K – Q3	K – Kt6
7. K – K3	K – Kt7
8. R – Kt4 ch	K – R6

Now the king is at the edge of the board and ready to be killed.

9. K – B3	K – R7
10. K – B2	K – R6
11. R – Q4!	

R – QR4, R – QKt4, QB4, K4, KB4, are equally good. This 'waiting move' forces the black king to go back to the fatal position directly opposite its white counterpart.

11. ...	K – R7
12. R – R4 mate.	

Mates are also possible with king and two bishops against a lone king, or with king, bishop, and knight, although not with king and two knights (barring a mistake by the weaker side). These mates are so rare that they are not worth the space ; the principle in both cases is to drive the king into the corner of the board with the aid of the king and the two minor pieces and there checkmate him.

PAWN PROMOTION

Quite often a closely-fought game will end up with a situation in which a king and one or two pawns are pitted against a lone king ; and then the question is whether the pawn can be made into a queen. A lone bishop or knight is not enough to force checkmate, so that you certainly cannot expect to checkmate with a pawn, the weakest unit on the chessboard.

An advantage of two pawns ahead is normally decisive, as witness the typical situation in Figure 35.

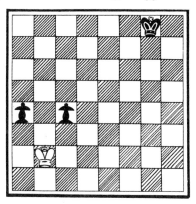

Fig. 35 – The king can only await events.

Here the king cannot approach either pawn, for if 1. K – B3, P – R6! ; 2. K × P?, P – R7 and Black queens. So 1. K – Kt1!, and now if Black incautiously replies 1. ..., P – R6? ; 2. K – R2, P – B6 ; 3. K × P, P – B7 ; 4. K – Kt2, and White captures both pawns. So 1. K – Kt1, K – B2! ; and Black brings his king over to shepherd the pawns through to queen.

THE SQUARE

In Figures 36A and 36B, the black king is too far away to help the pawn, so all depends on whether the white king can catch it or not. The easiest way to work out is *not* to say to yourself ' I go there, he goes there, I go there ' which is confusing, but to imagine a square drawn on the board with its side the line joining the square on which the pawn stands to its queening square. If you can move inside this square with your king on your first move, you will catch the pawn, but otherwise it queens. In Figure 36A, White cannot catch the pawn, even if it is his turn to move, while in 36B everything

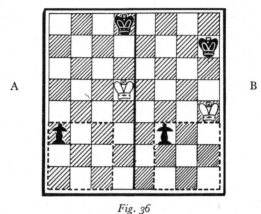

A   B

Fig. 36

depends on who is to move. White to move draws, Black to move wins.

KING IN FRONT OF THE PAWN

What happens when the lone king is barring the way to queen of the pawn ? In this case, the vital rule to remember, if you have the pawn, is to keep your king in FRONT of the pawn. In this way, you can drive the enemy king out of the way and queen the pawn ; if you advance the pawn first, the game is certainly drawn. Figure 37 shows the critical case.

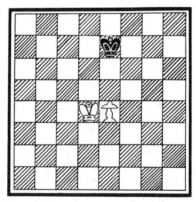

Fig. 37 – White to move wins.

First of all, see what happens if White does not put his king in front of the pawn. 1. P – K5?, K – K3! ; 2. K – K4, K – K2! (Black makes sure that *his* king stays in the right place); 3. K – Q5, K – Q2 (now Black's king bars the way to the white king, and he must again put his pawn forward first) ; 4. P – K6 ch, K – K2 ; 5. K – K5, K – K1! (again in front of the pawn) ; 6. K – Q6, K – Q1 (again barring the way) ; 7. P – K7 ch, K – K1 ; 8. K – K6, stalemate.

The same thing happens if White advances his king in the diagram, without advancing it in front of the pawn. 1. K – Q5?, K – Q2! (barring the way), 2. P – K5, K – K2 ; 3. P – K6, K – K1 ; 4. K – Q6, K – Q1 ; 5. P – K7 ch, K – K1 ; 6. K – K6, stalemate.

If White's king advances in front of the pawn in the diagram however, it is the black king whose way is barred and must retreat a rank : 1. K – K5!, K – K1 ; 2. K – K6! (again barring the way), K – Q1 ; 3. K – B7!, and now the pawn simply runs through to queen : 3. ..., K – Q2 ; 4. P – K5, K – Q1 ; 5. P – K6, K – B2 ; 6. P – K7. It is worth remembering, however, that if White's king can reach the sixth rank in front of the pawn, then the game is won even if it is White's turn to move and his way is barred. Thus, set up a position with white king on K6, pawn at K5 ; black king at K1. White to move wins by 1. K – Q6, K – Q1 ; 2. P – K6, K – K1 ; 3. P – K7, K – B2 ; 4. K – Q7.

This idea of barring the way to the opposing king is known in chess as 'the opposition'. In Figure 37, after White's initial move 1. K – K5, White has 'the opposition' as Black's king is forced to retreat. The opposition plays an important part in many endgames, as the king which can invade the enemy's position after securing the opposition and forcing the opponent to give ground can often secure a decisive advantage.

BEWARE OF THE ROOK'S PAWN

One ending with king and pawn against king which cannot be won is where a rook's pawn is involved. Even if White has the 'ideal' position with king at KR6, pawn at KR5, and the black king at KR1, with Black having to move and

thus lose the opposition, the ending is not to be won. 1. ...,
K – Kt1 ; 2. K – Kt6, K – R1 ; 3. P – R6, K – Kt1 ; 4.
P – R7 ch, K – R1 ; 5. K – R6 stalemate. The reason for
this ending being drawn and not won is that when Black
loses the opposition and gives ground, the square across
which the white king would advance forward is off the edge
of the board ; it doesn't exist !

Even an ending with king, bishop, and rook's pawn against
king is drawn if the bishop does not command the queening
square and the lone king can reach it.

Set up a position with the white K on QKt5, B on QB5,
P on QR6 ; Black K on QR1.

The continuation might be 1. K – Kt6, K – Kt1 ; 2. B – Q6
ch, K – R1 ; 3. P – R7, stalemate. Were the bishop a
white-squared one (thus commanding the queening square)
the ending would be easily won.

KING AND TWO PAWNS AGAINST KING AND PAWN

This ending is normally won fairly easily, the only exceptions
being normally where the extra pawn is doubled (doubled
pawns are pawns on the same file) or where a rook's pawn is
concerned. Even this is not invariable ; in Figure 38, Black
should win because his extra pawn is passed (a passed pawn
has no enemy pawn on the same or the adjacent file to hinder
it from queening) and because his king is well placed.

Fig. 38 – Black to move wins.

The winning line is 1. ..., K – K5. (not 1. ..., K – K6 ; 2. K – Kt3!, K – K7 ; 3. K – Kt2, when Black cannot make progress because White has the opposition and bars the way) ; 2. K – Kt3, K – K6 ; 3. K – Kt2, K – K7 ; 4. K – Kt3 (if 4. K – Kt1, K – B6 ; 5. K – B1, K – Kt6 and wins the RP), K – B8 ; 5. K – R2, K – B7 (notice how Black still keeps the opposition) ; 6. K – R1, K – Kt6 (but not 6. ..., P – Kt6?? stalemate) ; and wins.

In the actual game, which took place in a Hungarian ladies' tournament, Black suffered a rush of blood to the head and hastily moved 1. ..., P – Kt6?? (violating the rule that the king should go in front of the pawn where possible) ; 2. K – R3!, and Black had nothing better than 2. ..., K – B6 ; stalemate.

Chapter Six

THE VALUE OF THE PIECES

FOR THE BEGINNER, it is a good idea to keep in mind a rough assessment of the relative value of each piece. Until you have been playing for quite some time, you will find it very difficult to plan any general strategy in your games, and your main concern will be to avoid blunders which lose your pieces unnecessarily and to take advantage of any such mistakes by your opponent. It is because the major pieces (the queens and rooks) are more valuable than the minor pieces (bishops and knights) that it is unwise to bring out your queen and rooks to exposed advanced positions early in the game. For if your opponent replies correctly he will be able to harry these pieces with his bishops, knights, and pawns. As pieces are exchanged and the board becomes less crowded, the opportunities for the wide-ranging major pieces becomes steadily greater.

In reckoning the value of the pieces, the pawn, the weakest unit on the board, may be counted as 1. In these terms, the other pieces can be assessed as follows :

Queen	9
Rook	5
Bishop	$3\frac{1}{2}$
Knight	3

The king, being priceless, cannot be suitably fitted into this reckoning, and there are other important modifications according to how far the game has progressed. In any case, it is clear that much depends on the position of the opposing forces, for it is not much use having a material advantage if you are mated. Allowing for this, it is worth while keeping in mind the following considerations when you find yourself with one of the fairly common cases of unbalanced material.

A. A piece against two, three, or four pawns.

A piece should almost always win against two pawns, except

possibly in the ending when the pawns are far advanced. Three pawns are practically never worth a piece in the opening, unless they form a central pawn mass or are combined with a lead in development. In the middle game, three pawns are unlikely to be worth a piece unless at least two of them are well advanced, united (united pawns are pawns on adjacent files which support each other) and passed ; and even then, the player a piece down must have enough remaining pieces around in the area of his pawns to support their advance. In the ending three pawns normally outweigh a piece unless they are very far back, or else if they are doubled, isolated, or otherwise open to easy attack by the player with the piece.

Four pawns outweigh a piece in most circumstances, unless the player with the extra piece can utilise it in an attack on the king or unless the pawns are weak and easily subject to attack.

B. The Exchange against a pawn or two pawns.

The phrase ' to win the exchange ' means to win a rook for a knight or bishop. However, since the rook is a piece which increases in effectiveness as pieces are exchanged and the ending approaches, the advantage of the exchange normally is greater the fewer pieces there are on the board. For instance, in the opening, there are some cases in which the exchange is deliberately sacrificed in order to gain time for a counter-attack. In the middle game, two bishops and a pawn sometimes outweigh a rook and a knight, particularly when the bishops are covering parallel diagonals. Generally, two bishops in combination are much more effective than two knights or than bishop and knight, which is one reason why the bishop is rated a slightly better piece than the knight.

Sometimes, situations occur in which a rook can be sacrificed for a knight or a bishop and one or two pawns. This favours the rook in the middle game and endgame except where the minor piece is very well posted or the pawns are central ones or are far advanced.

C. Three pieces against a queen.

Although the mathematical rating of three minor pieces
(9½ or 10) is little different to that of the queen (9) or two
rooks (10), in practice the pieces are usually superior, except
when they are scattered or their king is exposed, thus allowing
the queen to do some damage by means of forks or other
attacks.

D. Two minor pieces against rook, rook and pawn, or rook and two pawns.

An opening line sometimes chosen by very inexperienced
players with White is 1. P – K4, P – K4 ; 2. Kt – KB3,
Kt – QB3 ; 3. B – B4, B – B4 ; 4. P – Q3, Kt – B3 ; 5. Kt –
Kt5?, Castles ; 6. Kt × BP?, R × Kt ; 7. B × R ch, K × B.
In other words, two minor pieces are given up for a rook and
a pawn, generally under the impression that White is securing
something like a material equivalent. But in the opening
stages, the rook has very little scope, while the minor pieces
have plenty ; during the early part of the game, therefore,
two minor pieces outweigh rook and pawn, usually rook and
two pawns, and possibly even rook and three pawns.

As the game develops, so the situation alters. The rook's
scope improves as exchanges take place, and in a middle
game with five or six pieces on each side as well as the pawns,
rook and pawn against two minor pieces is a pretty level
battle. The exception is again two bishops, which are easily
worth rook and two pawns.

In the endgame, the rook is in its element, and not only
do rook and pawn slightly outweigh two minor pieces, but
even the rook on its own may do fairly well, always assuming
that the two minor pieces are not two bishops.

The novice should not try to remember all the generalisations in this chapter and commit them to memory ; for you
will certainly find that in the great majority of your games
during your first few months of playing chess, the forces are
never of the fine graduations described in this chapter. But
the principle involved if you have a vast variation in the
strength of the opposing forces, such as a queen against a
bishop, or two rooks for two bishops, is simple : SWAP,

SWAP, and SWAP some more. There is an entirely fallacious idea among some weak players that it is ' unsporting ' to exchange pieces when you have a material advantage, and such players will be particularly indignant if you exchange. Such ideas are quite wrong. If you want to improve at chess, it is essential to acquire the technique of winning positions where you have a material advantage ; and this technique is simply to eliminate the remaining enemy pieces until they are so few in number that they are unable to resist a checkmating attack or the queening of a pawn. Once you can win efficiently when you are a piece ahead against an opponent of equal strength, you become the more capable of dealing with the harder problems involved in evaluating an extra pawn or two, and finally of exploiting the more subtle nuances described in this chapter.

Chapter Seven

GENERAL ADVICE : THE OPENING

During your first games of chess, you will certainly be completely bewildered by the apparently limitless number of possibilities available at every move. How on earth do you decide between one move and another ? Neither I nor any other writer can tell you a specific way of deciding this in any particular position ; what you can do is to keep in mind a number of general principles about the best methods of utilising each particular piece, and the types of traps and stratagems which most often lead to mates and winning of material.

A strong player approaches a chess game, once the opening is over, with the idea of forming a general plan of campaign ; a king's side attack, an outflanking movement on the queen's side, pressure against pawn weaknesses in the enemy camp, exchange into an ending in order to increase permanent positional advantages, and so on. But until you have enough experience to draw upon to form such general plans, you have on the whole to concentrate on more short-term ideas like winning your opponent's pieces and avoiding losing yours. The master, of course, also has to take account of these immediate considerations in carrying out his long-term ideas, and has constantly to modify these ideas because of the tactical opportunities which crop up.

This will not satisfy some readers who would like to know whether it is better to play attacking chess and aim at the opponent's king as soon as possible, or whether they should rather take matters more cautiously and concentrate on preserving a solid situation. As your chess improves, you will find that your own preferences become apparent, and your style will form itself, but in the early stages of your acquaintance with chess it is very important to try all the time to do something constructive and positive. Only in this way will you get the feel of what the pieces can do and gain the understanding of what types of plan are valid in various positions. If you play completely negatively, you may win more games in the beginning, but in the long run your game will suffer.

Playing constructively, however, doesn't mean that you have to be looking for ways to attack the enemy king all the time. If you don't see any tactical threats in a position either to your opponent's pieces or to your own, you should look for ways of increasing the mobility of your pieces and controlling more of the board. Unless the other man plays very badly, you won't have a chance of mounting a successful attack on the king until quite late in the game.

If you're a very weak player, however, it's very likely that either you and your opponent will win some considerable amount of material, say a piece, quite early on because of an oversight by the other side. If it is your opponent that makes such a blunder, then this immediately determines your general strategy FOR THE ENTIRE GAME THEREAFTER. If you think this sounds far-fetched, look at Figures 39 and 40.

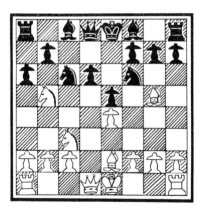

Fig. 39 – A typical beginner's blunder ; White plays Castles??, allowing the reply ..., P × Kt. From now on, Black should aim at exchanging his pieces for his opponent's (assuming that equal material is being exchanged) as often as possible. For the result, see the next diagram.

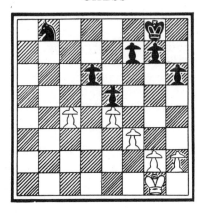

*Fig. 40 – The result, some thirty moves
later. Now Black wins easily (a) by
attacking the QBP with his knight and
king and so winning it, (b) by bringing his
king to K3, his knight to Q5, and his KKtP
to KKt3, (c) by playing P – KB4, forcing
White to reply KP × KBP (otherwise
Black himself plays KBP × KP and wins
the isolated KP by attacking it with king
and knight), (d) by advancing his passed
QP through to Queen, supported by the king
and knight.*

These two diagrams explain why you should exchange
when material ahead. In the first case, there are many
pieces on the board and White has all sorts of attacks himself ;
in the second, White can offer no effective hindrance to
Black's winning plan (all he can do is to wriggle his king
backwards and forwards). This can be put in mathematical
terms ; in the first diagram, after Black captures the knight,
his advantage in material (counting the queen as 9, the rook
as 5, and so on) is 39 against 36 ; in the second, it is 8 against
5. In other words, as you bring about exchanges, your
material advantage becomes proportionately greater.

Now a word of warning. Some games are lost because
players, after gaining a material advantage, just do nothing
and wait for the game to win itself. Winning material

should not result in playing passively ; you should continue when there is no tactical opportunity in the position, to look for ways of improving the position of your pieces and increasing your control of the board. In fact, continuing to play in this way will ensure that you bring about your desired exchanges ; for if your pieces become posted on advanced squares with plenty of scope, your opponent will find himself left with no choice but to exchange them or allow you increased opportunities for attack.

What if you have been so unfortunate as to make a blunder like White's in Figure 39 ? In this case, the converse applies. You should, on the whole, avoid exchanges, unless they enhance the scope of your remaining pieces and make your opponent's cramped and passive.

So much for considerations which a beginner should keep in mind for the whole game ; the rest of this chapter, together with the next two chapters, consists of general advice for each part of the game.

THE OPENING

Two principles are paramount in the opening : the DEVELOPMENT of the pieces on to squares where they are in good action, and the control of the CENTRE of the board. The importance attached to the central squares is because it is from these that the pieces have the greatest scope. In addition, if you control the centre you can use it as a clearing-house from which the pieces can be sent to either wing. If your opponent controls the centre, you will find that your pieces take longer to get from one side of the board to the other, and that they become cramped and get in each other's way. Developing the pieces has two objects : to get these pieces into play, and to clear the back line for the rooks. The rooks are best posted on the back lines on the king's, queen's or bishop's files ; when they are in satisfactory positions, development is completed.

If you can get your pieces into play quicker than your opponent, you have the right to take the initiative in the next part of the game ; and so it follows that, where possible, you should get each piece out in one move. It is rarely good to move a piece twice in the opening, except to save it from capture or to make an important capture yourself.

In practice, the bishops are the hardest pieces to develop. In most cases the knights belong at B3, where they command two of the four central squares. More rarely, they can go to K2 or Q2. Make it a rule NEVER to develop a knight at R3 ; there are a few openings where this development is playable, but even in these B3 or K or Q2 are equally good alternatives.

The ideal situation for the pawns in the opening is to have the two centre ones abreast on Q4 and K4. If you ever have the chance to reach this formation without one pawn being exchanged, do so. Normally, however, your opponent will have the same idea of occupying the centre as you, so the formation is rarely possible. As a substitute, keep in mind the following rule : *If you play P – K4 on the first move, leave yourself the option of playing P – Q4 at a later stage ; if you play P – Q4 on the first move, leave yourself the option of P – QB4.* In the first case, you will normally have to advance P – Q4 unsupported by a pawn, although there are some openings in which you can play P – QB3 (preparing P – Q4) and delay the development of your QKt. In the second group of openings (P – Q4 on the first move) the important thing to remember is NOT to block the QBP with the knight. This applies whether you are White or Black.

P – QB4 is also a reasonable opening move (usually followed up by P – Q4) but inexperienced players are recommended to avoid openings involving P – KB4 at an early stage, since the king is too liable to become exposed.

The bishops form one of the major problems in development. They have usually a choice of squares in the various types of opening, which can best be expressed in tabular form.

	White KB	White QB	Black KB	Black QB
KP openings (1. P – K4, P – K4)	(1) QB4 (bearing on KB7, which is only defended by the K) (2) QKt5.	(1) KKt5 (pinning Black KKt) ; but delay doing this until Black has castled.	(1) K2. (2) QB4.	(1) K3 (2) KKt5 (if the white KKt can be pinned).

In all the above openings, both sides should normally develop the QB last of the four minor pieces, until it is clear what formation the opponent will adopt.

1. P – K4 by White ; other first moves by Black.	(1) QKt5 once the black QKt is out) (2) Q3 (if White can play P – K5)	(1) KKt5. (2) K3.	(1) K2. (2) QKt5. (3) KKt2.	(1) Q2. (2) KKt5 (if the pin on White's KKt is effective)
QP openings (1. P – Q4, P – Q4)	(1) Q3. (2) KKt2 (after White has played P – KKt3).	(1) KKt5. (2) QKt2.	(1) K2. (2) QKt5.	(1) Keep at QB1 until there is a chance to free your game with ..., P – K4. (2) QKt2.
QP openings without 1. ..., P – Q4 by Black.	(1) Q3. (2) If Black fianchettoes his KB by ...,P–KKt3 B – Kt2, then White should put his own bishop at K2 or KKt2.	(1) K3. (2) KKt5. (3) Where White plays an early P – K3, this B stays at home or is fianchettoed.	(1) QKt5 (where the white QKt can be pinned) (2) KKt2.	(1) KKt5 (when the other bishop is fianchettoed) (2) QKt2 (when the KB is at QKt5)

These generalisations about the bishops are the most liable to exceptions of all the pieces, so do not take them as gospel, but only as a guide. Experience will teach you that if you put bishops on other squares than those mentioned in each type of opening, they will often become vulnerable to attack by the enemy's pawns or knights.

The general principles involved in bringing out the other pieces are considerably simpler. The inexperienced player should always *castle on the king's side*. There are situations where queen's side castling can be followed by a king's side attack, but they demand exact handling and the beginner who attempts them is likely to find that the more exposed position of his king on the queen's side leads to trouble.

Once you have castled king's side, where do you put your rooks ? Not just on any centre file, but preferably behind a pawn which is likely to advance, be exchanged, and thus give the rook the open line which it really wants.

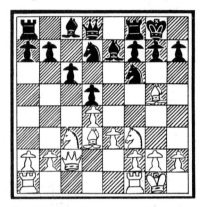

Fig. 41 – Rook development : Black plays ..., R – K1 and White replies QR – Kt1.

Figure 41 is a typical example. The reason for Black's move ..., R – K1 is fairly obvious : the rook is going to the only file which is not blocked by a black pawn. Later on, the rook will support the black knight advancing to a better post at K5. White's QR – Kt1 is more subtle. He intends to open a line for the rook by P – QKt4 and P – Kt5 ; later on in the game, the white pieces can invade along this open line. The file already clear of white pawns, the QB file, is reserved for the KR, which will thus also support the white QKt if it manoeuvres to a better post at QB5 via QR4. Why does not White open a line for a rook by KR – K1, followed by P – K4 ? This would not be bad, but it would have the disadvantage, after White's P – K4 and Black's reply ..., P × P, of leaving White's QP isolated (unprotected by other pawns) and subject to attack.

There is one rule only for the queen in the opening ; don't bring her out too early. It is true that there are some elementary traps, which have occurred thousands of times in beginners' games (see page 71) in which the queen is brought out early ; but once these traps are avoided, the queen is driven around by the enemy minor pieces with great loss of time.

Finally, here is a miscellaneous list of what to avoid in the opening :

1. *Don't* play P – KR4 or P – QR4 and try to bring your rooks into play via R3. For one thing, they will probably get captured by the enemy bishops ; rooks belong behind pawns in the opening, not in front of them.

2. *Don't* play either of your RPs to R3 to stop the enemy bishop coming to Kt5. It is surprising the number of even quite experienced players who do this, but it is generally a complete waste of time.

3. *Don't* capture a pawn at the cost of time which you could otherwise spend in development. This applies particularly to wing pawns ; a centre pawn can sometimes be captured with the object, not of keeping it, but of making the opponent use up valuable time to regain it. Here's an example of unsound pawn snatching : 1. P – Q4, Kt – KB3 ; 2. P – QB4, P – KKt3 ; 3. Kt – QB3, B – Kt2 ; 4. P – K4, P – Q3 ; 5. P – B4, Castles ; 6. Kt – B3, P – B4 ; 7. B – K2, P × P ; 8. Kt × P, Kt – B3 ; 9. Kt – B2. Here Black should continue his development by 9. ..., B – Q2, but instead plays 9. ..., Q – Kt3? ; 10. B – K3, Q × P? ; 11. Kt – R4, and the queen is trapped. It is notoriously risky to capture the QKtP with the queen.

Now an example of capturing a centre pawn to make the opponent lose time : 1. P – K4, P – K4 ; 2. Kt – KB3, Kt – QB3 ; 3. B – B4, Kt – B3 ; 4. P – Q4, P × P ; 5. Castles, Kt × P ; 6. R – K1, P – Q4 ; 7. B × P, Q × B ; 8. Kt – B3, Q – QR4 ; 9. Kt × Kt, B – K3 ; 10. Kt (K4) – Kt5, Castles ; 11. Kt × B, P × Kt ; 12. R × P, B – Q3. White has regained both the lost pawns, but while he was doing so, Black has completed his development and has a good position.

4. A positional error which is very common among the inexperienced is to support a centre pawn threatened with

exchange with a knight. This allows the opponent full control of the centre, e.g. 1. P – Q4, P – Q4 ; 2. P – QB4, Kt – KB3? (Black should give his QP pawn support by P – K3 or P – QB3) ; 3. P × P, Kt × P ; 4. P – K4, Kt – Kt3 ; 5. Kt – QB3, and White has the ideal formation of two pawns abreast in the centre.

Another example : 1. P – K4, P – K4 ; 2. P – Q4, Kt – QB3? ; 3. P × P, Kt × P ; 4. P – KB4, Kt – Kt3 ; 5. B – B4, B – K2 ; 6. Kt – QB3, and again White has the upper hand in the centre.

TYPICAL OPENINGS

A great temptation, both to the novice and to the more experienced player who ought to know better, is to concentrate on the openings at the sacrifice of study of other parts of the game. The openings are easier to read up than the middle game or ending, but it is quite useless getting an advantage at the beginning if your opponent proceeds to outplay you later on. The worst thing of all is to learn variations off by heart, for, once the opponent deviates from what you know, you will be completely stumped.

So until you have acquired a fair amount of experience, you shouldn't try to learn up openings ; the principles outlined in this chapter will assure you a satisfactory position from the opening against any but strong players.

Here are two examples of fairly common openings, one with the king's pawn and one with the queen's pawn.

The Hungarian Defence.

1. P – K4	P – K4
2. Kt – KB3	Kt – QB3
3. B – B4	B – K2

This is a safer move for the beginner to adopt than 3. ..., B – B4, when he may have to contend with either the Evans Gambit 4. P – QKt4 or with 4. P – B3, which also starts quite a dangerous attack. It also avoids the pitfalls of the other obvious move, 3. ..., Kt – B3 ; when 4. Kt – Kt5 is very

trappy (Black's best answer is to sacrifice a pawn by 4. ...,
P – Q4 ; 5. P × P, Kt – Q5 ; but this is complicated).

| 4. Castles | P – Q3 |

Preparing to develop the QB. 4. ..., Kt – B3 is also good,
for now if 5. Kt – Kt5?, Castles ; and White has simply lost
time with his knight.

| 5. P – B3 | Kt – B3 |
| 6. R – K1 | |

White places his rook on a centre file and at the same time
defends his KP.

| 6. ... | Castles |

Another playable move is 6. ..., B – Kt5 ; pinning the white
knight. Less good is 6. ..., B – K3 ; for White replies 7. B ×
B, P × B ; and Black has doubled pawns which are weak.

| 7. P – Q4 | |

White places a second pawn in the centre, and prepares to
develop his QB and QKt.

| 7. ... | B – Kt5! |

Here this pin is very good, for White cannot answer 8. P –
KR3, B × Kt ; 9. Q × B (developing) because he loses a
pawn by 9. ..., P × P ; 10. P × P, Kt × QP. He must
instead reply 9. P × B, when the pawn defences in front of
his king are in ruins.

| 8. P – Q5 | |

Black threatened 8. ..., B × Kt in any case ; and if 8. QKt –
Q2, he can take advantage of the pin to win a pawn by
8. ..., P × P ; 9. P × P, Kt × QP. Since 8. B – K3 the
only other way of giving the QP extra protection, is met by
8. ..., Kt × KP ; White's actual move is practically forced.

| 8. ... | Kt – Kt1 |

An interesting moment ; at first sight Black has gone wrong,
for his knight has had to retreat to its original square. But
the loss of time is compensated for by the fact that P – Q5 has
considerably reduced the scope of White's bishop, which is

now blocked by a pawn. Secondly, Black's QB4 square is no longer controlled by a white pawn, and Black hopes that his knight may eventually be able to reach it (via Q2) and thus attack the white KP.

9.	QKt – Q2	QKt – Q2
10.	Kt – B1	

White intends to bring his knight round to K3 or KKt3, so that it can, later on, go to an advanced outpost at KB5.

10.	...	R – K1

Although the rook has no more scope here than at KB1, Black wants to make room for his own knight to come on to the king's side. He abandons the alternative idea of ..., Kt – B4 because White can simply drive the knight away by Kt – Kt3 (protecting the KP a second time), followed by P – QKt4.

11.	Kt – Kt3	Kt – B1
12.	P – KR3	

An alternative is 13. Kt – B5, B × Kt ; 14. P × B. White would then have exchanged off one of the black bishops, but on the other hand he has the weakness of doubled KBPs.

12.	...	B – Q2

This is a typical blocked position ; nothing has been exchanged, and the further development of the game depends on long manoeuvres by either side. Black might now, for instance, play ..., P – QB3 in order to exchange White's advanced pawn and himself gain space for attack on the queen's side. A likely plan for White is Kt – R2, R – KB1, P – KB4, and a gradual advance of all the pawns on the king's side. There is plenty of scope for both players.

The Queen's Gambit.

1.	P – Q4

This and 1. P – K4 are equally popular as opening moves.

1.	...	P – Q4
2.	P – QB4	P – K3

Although this opening is called the Queen's Gambit, it is very bad for Black to accept it and then try to hold on to the pawn. One typical possibility is 2. ..., P × P ; 3. P – K3, P – QKt4 ; 4. P – QR4, P – QB3 ; 5. P × P, P × P ; 6. Q – B3, winning a piece.

3. Kt – KB3		Kt – KB3
4. P – K3		

4. B – Kt5, pinning the knight, is also good here, as is 4. Kt – B3.

4. ...		B – K2
5. Kt – B3		Castles
6. B – Q3		

In most QP openings, this is the right square for the white KB ; it bears down on KR7, one of the weak spots in Black's castled position.

6. ...	QKt – Q2

Kt – QB3 is rarely good in QP openings when the knight blocks the QBP.

7. Castles	P – QKt3
8. P – QKt3	B – Kt2
9. B – Kt2	P – B4
10. R – B1	

A case where the rook is developed to a square where it anticipates the opening of a file ; it is virtually certain that the opposing QBP and QPs will be exchanged in due course, and when that happens the rook's scope will be enhanced.

10. ...	R – B1
11. Q – K2	Q – B2

Both sides unite their rooks.

12. KR – Q1	

The queen's file, like the QB file, will benefit a rook once the centre pawns are exchanged.

12. ...	KR – Q1

Here the development on both sides has been more straight-forward than in the previous openings. All the pieces are in play, but White has maintained the advantage of the first move. Thus, Black's queen is slightly worse placed than White's because it is on the same line as a hostile rook. To leave your queen on the same file as an enemy rook or the same diagonal as an enemy bishop often spells danger ; in this case Black will probably have to spend another move to remove his queen from danger by ..., Q – Kt1. In addition, White's knight at QB3 is slightly more aggressive than Black's at Q2. However, these are minor advantages and in practice the position is almost even.

DEFENDING AGAINST 1 P – Q4 AND UNORTHODOX OPENINGS

Many inexperienced players become alarmed when their opponent does something other than the normal moves 1. P – Q4 and 1. P – K4. It is a great time-saver to know, as the famous Australian master Cecil Purdy once pointed out, that against any unorthodox openings, as well as against 1. P – Q4, you can reply, as Black, with the same five initial moves and emerge with a reasonable game.

1.	P – Q4	P – Q4
2.	P – QB4	P – K3

If White opens with 1. P – QB4, then not 1. ..., P – Q4? because of 2. P × P, Q × P ; 3. Kt – QB3, and Black's queen has been brought out too early, but 1. ..., P – K3 ; and only after 2. P – Q4 (or 2. Kt – QB3 or 2. Kt – KB3). 2. ..., P – Q4. The other important modification to this 'all-purpose' system for Black is that after 1. P – Q4, P – Q4 ; 2. Kt – KB3 or 2. P – K3, Black plays 2. ..., Kt – KB3! before ..., P – K3. The reason is to stop White getting in to the 'Colle Opening' 1. P – Q4, P – Q4 ; 2. Kt – KB3, P – K3 ; 3. P – K3, Kt – KB3 ; 4. B – Q3, B – K2 ; Castles, in which White doesn't play P – QB4 but prepares for P – K4. Against the Colle, Black's best line is 1. P – Q4, P – Q4 ; 2. Kt – KB3, Kt – KB3 ; 3. P – K3, P – KKt3! ; 4. B – Q3, B – Kt2 ; the bishop at Q3 isn't nearly so effective when confronted with a fianchettoed position. If Black is going to play ..., P – KKt3, he doesn't need ..., P – K3 as well.

However, after 1. P – Q4, P – Q4 ; 2. P – QB4, Black shouldn't play 2. ..., Kt – KB3 because of 3. P × P, Kt × P ; 3. P – K4! and White controls the centre (see page 64).

      3. Kt – KB3

The same next three moves for Black are also playable against the normal Queen's Gambit line 3. Kt – QB3 and 4. B – Kt5.

3. ...	Kt – KB3
4. P – K3	B – K2
5. B – Q3	Castles

All these five black moves are always reasonably good against ANY opening apart from 1. P – K4. Of course, should White offer a pawn or a piece for nothing, interrupt the system and take it, e.g. 1. P – KKt4 (the 'Spike' Opening), P – Q4 ; and if White now fails to protect his KKtP, then 2. ..., B × P.

Now let us assume that White continues as in the last opening (Queen's Gambit) which we discussed ; can Black improve his play ?

      6. Kt – B3   P – B4

This move can be played early, and thus allow a more aggressive development of Black's QKt than at Q2.

      7. Castles   QP × P

Making this capture here allows a more effective development of Black's pieces than waiting till White has played P – QKt3 and can recapture with the pawn.

8. B × P	P – QKt3
9. P – QKt3	B – Kt2
10. B – Kt2	P × P

10. ..., QKt – Q2 and 10. ..., Kt – B3 are both quite good, but the actual move gives White a rather weak isolated pawn if he recaptures with the pawn here. The pros and cons of such an isolated pawn are one of the eternal subjects of chess controversy ; some maintaining that the extra control of

the board resulting from a pawn on a good central square outweighs the vulnerability of the pawn, others the opposite.

| 11. Kt × P | Kt – B3 |
| 12. Kt × Kt | |

An interesting moment ; if White allows Black to exchange knights (12. ..., Kt × Kt ; 13. P × Kt) his isolated pawn is weaker than on the previous move, because the exchange of a pair of pieces has moved the position a step nearer the ending. Fixed weaknesses like an isolated pawn are easiest to exploit in an ending, because the scarcity of material makes it harder for the side having the weakness to create a diversion elsewhere on the board.

12. ...	B × Kt
13. Q – K2	Q – B2
14. KR – Q1	KR – Q1
15. QR – B1	QR – B1

Both sides have completed their development and the game is even.

DON'T MEMORISE!

Now an awful warning for beginners ; don't try to memorise these openings and to play them by rote ; they are just a very few of many thousands of reasonable ways of beginning a game. When you play them over, note the ways in which the various pieces are brought into positions where they influence the centre, and keep this in view as an objective in your own openings. When you have White or Black, it is worth while trying out the general strategy in the openings given here, and after you have played a number of games, you can try looking up the openings in one of the textbooks on this subject (see Chapter 12) and seeing how masters' play has differed from your own. But when you play over the opening moves of a game between masters, don't take their moves as gospel. On most occasions in any opening there is more than one reasonable alternative, and what you should look for is the way in which particular moves fit into the strategy of the opening as a whole.

Chapter Eight

OPENING TRAPS YOU SHOULD KNOW

IN THE LAST chapter I said that you should not try to memorise opening variations. There are, however, a number of common traps in various openings which owe their sting to the fact that the loser's moves are quite natural. If you are a complete beginner, you are unlikely to find opportunities to set any of them (or fall into them !) except the first two. But when you have reached a rather more advanced level, you will find quite a few opponents who play ' book ' openings without knowing a great deal about them. Against these, it is worth while trying for the traps given below if you have the chance, since in no case (except the first two) do you have to make bad moves to reach the trapping position.

Trap No. 1. Scholar's Mate – the bane of all beginners. 1. P – K4, P – K4 ; 2. B – B4, Kt – QB3 (simpler is 2. ..., Kt – KB3 ; then if 3. Q – R5??, Kt × Q) ; 3. Q – R5, Kt – KB3?? ; 4. Q × P mate.

Trap No. 2 – The Advanced Scholar's Trap. 1. P – K4, P – K4 ; 2. B – B4, B – B4 ; 3. Q – R5, P – KKt3?? ; 4. Q × P ch, Q – K2 ; 5. Q × R, and wins. A simpler answer to both Nos. 1 and 2 is 1. P – K4, P – K4 ; 2. B – B4, B – B4 ; 3. Q – R5, Q – K2. Next move, you play 4. ..., Kt – KB3 ; attacking the white queen and driving it back, after which Black is well ahead in development and has the advantage.

Trap No. 3 – Waste of time by P – R3. This is not a trap that has any definite order of moves, but since it exemplifies a type of strategy prevalent among weak players, it is well worth including. 1. P – K4, P – K4 ; 2. Kt – KB3, Kt – QB3 ; 3. B – B4, B – B4 ; 4. Kt – B3 (Giuoco Piano Opening), P – Q3 ; 5. P – Q3, Kt – B3 ; 6. P – KR3?, Castles ; 7. P – R3? (as far as I know, the type of player who makes these moves in the opening intends P – KR3 to stop ..., B – KKt5,

P – QR3 to start a queen's side attack. Both ideas are bad.), Kt – K2! (the simplest way to take advantage ; Black intends a king's side attack) ; 8. Castles, Kt – Kt3 ; 9. P – QKt4, B – Kt3 ; 10. B – Kt2?, Kt – B5! (exploiting White's P – KR3; now the knight cannot be driven away without loss of a pawn) ; 11. Q – Q2, Kt(B3) – R4 ; 12. QR – Q1, Q – B3 ; 13. Kt – Q5, Kt × Kt ; 14. P × Kt, Kt – B5 ; 15. KR – K1, B × RP! ; 16. P × B, Q – Kt3 ch ; 17. K – R2, Q – Kt7 mate. The exact moves may vary, but this kind of attack should settle the hash of the double P – R3 man.

Trap No. 4 – Petroff Defence. 1. P – K4, P – K4 ; 2. Kt – KB3, Kt – KB3 ; 3. Kt × P, Kt × P?? (P – Q3 first is right) ; 4. Q – K2, Kt – KB3 ; 5. Kt – B6 dis. ch., winning the queen.

Trap No. 5 – Ruy Lopez – the Noah's Ark Trap. Not quite so old as it sounds, but pretty well-worn. 1. P – K4, P – K4 ; 2. Kt – KB3, Kt – QB3 ; 3. B – Kt5, P – QR3 ; 4. B – R4, P – Q3 ; 5. P – Q4, P – QKt4 ; 6. B – Kt3, Kt × P ; 7. Kt × Kt, P × Kt ; 8. Q × P? (8. P – QB3 is correct), P – QB4! ; 9. Q – Q5, B – K3 ; 10. Q – B6 ch, B – Q2 ; 11. Q – Q5, P – B5 ; and Black wins the bishop.

Trap No. 6 – Two Knights' Defence. 1. P – K4, P – K4 ; 2. Kt – KB3, Kt – QB3 ; 3. B – B4, Kt – B3 ; 4. Kt – Kt5, P – Q4 ; 5. P × P, Kt × P? (Kt – QR4 or Kt – Q5 are better) ; 6. P – Q4!, P × P ; 7. Castles, B – K2 ; 8. Kt × BP!, K × Kt ; 9. Q – B3 ch, K – K3 ; 10. Kt – B3!, P × Kt ; 11. R – K1 ch, Kt – K4 ; 12. B – B4, B – B3 ; 13. B × Kt, B × B ; 14. R × B ch!, K × R ; 15. R – K1 ch, K – Q5 ; 16. B × Kt, Q × B ; 17. R – Q1 ch, and wins.

Trap No. 7 – Vienna Gambit. 1. P – K4, P – K4 ; 2. Kt – QB3, Kt – KB3 ; 3. P – B4, P × P? (3. ..., P – Q4 is the only good move here) ; 4. P – K5, Q – K2 ; 5. Q – K2, Kt – Kt1 ; 6. Kt – B3, and White's advantage is overwhelming. One game continued 6. ..., Kt – QB3 ; 7. P – Q4, P – Q3 ; 8. Kt – Q5, Q – Q1 ; 9. Kt × P ch!, K – Q2 ; 10. Kt × R, P – B3 ; 11. B × P, KKt – K2 ; 12. P × QP, Kt – B4 ; 13. P – Q5, Kt(B3) – Q5 ; 14. Q – K6 ch!, Kt × Q ; 15. B – Kt5 mate.

Trap No. 8 – Sicilian Defence. 1. P – K4, P – QB4 ; 2. Kt – KB3, Kt – QB3 ; 3. P – Q4, P × P ; 4. Kt × P, Kt – B3 ; 5. Kt – QB3, P – Q3 ; 6. B – QB4, P –KKt3 ? (correct are 6. ..., P – K3 or 6. ..., B – Q2) ; 7. Kt × Kt, P × Kt ; 8. P – K5, P × P? ; 9. B × P ch!, K × B ; 10. Q × Q. An example of a ' tie ' combination (see Chapter 9) ; Black's king is tied to guarding both the KBP and the queen, and can be deflected with fatal results.

Trap No. 9 – Sicilian Defence. 1. P – K4, P – QB4 ; 2. Kt – KB3, P – Q3 ; 3. P – Q4, P × P ; 4. Kt × P, Kt – KB3 ; 5. Kt – QB3, P – KKt3 ; 6. P – B4, B – Kt2? (6. ..., Kt – B3 is right) ; 7. P – K5, P × P ; 8. P × P, Kt – Kt5 ; 9. B – Kt5 ch, K – B1 (if 9. ..., B – Q2 ; 10. Q × Kt) ; 10. Kt – K6 ch!, and wins the queen.

Trap No. 10 – Caro-Kann Defence. 1. P – K4, P – QB3 ; 2. P – Q4, P – Q4 ; 3. Kt – QB3, P × P ; 4. Kt × P, Kt – Q2 ; 5. Q – K2, KKt – B3?? ; 6. Kt – Q6 mate. This trap was once pulled off in an international masters tournament !

Trap No. 11 – Caro-Kann Defence. 1. P – K4, P – QB3 ; 2. Kt – QB3, P – Q4 ; 3. Kt – B3, P × P ; 4. Kt × P, B – B4? (4. ..., B – Kt5 or 4. ..., Kt – B3 are better) ; 5. Kt – Kt3, B – Kt3 ; 6. P – KR4, P – KR3 ; 7. Kt – K5, B – R2 ; 8. B – B4, P – K3 ; 9. Q – R5, P – KKt3 ; 10. Q – K2, Kt – B3 ; 11. Kt × KBP!, K × Kt ; 12. Q × P ch, K – Kt2 ; 13. Q – B7 mate.

Trap No. 12 – French Defence. 1. P – K4, P – K3 ; 2. P – Q4, P – Q4 ; 3. P – K5, P – QB4 ; 4. P – QB3, Kt – QB3 ; 5. Kt – KB3, Q – Kt3 ; 6. B – Q3, P × P ; 7. P × P, Kt × QP? (7. ..., B – Q2!) ; 8. Kt × Kt, Q × Kt ; 9. B – Kt5 ch, and wins the queen.

Trap No. 13 – Queen's Gambit Declined. 1. P – Q4, P – Q4 ; 2. P – QB4, P – K3 ; 3. Kt – QB3, Kt – KB3 ; 4. B – Kt5, QKt – Q2 ; 5. P × P, P × P ; 6. Kt × P?, Kt × Kt! ; 7. B × Q, B – Kt5 ch ; 8. Q – Q2, B × Q ch ; 9. K × B, K × B ; and Black has won a piece.

Trap No. 14 – Queen's Gambit Declined. 1. P – Q4,

P – Q4 ; 2. P – QB4, P – K3 ; 3. Kt – QB3, Kt – KB3 ; 4. B – Kt5, QKt – Q2 ; 5. P – K3, P – B3 ; 6. Kt – B3, Q – R4 ; 7. Q – B2, Kt – K5 ; 8. B – Q3? (8. B – B4 is better), Kt × B ; 9. Kt × Kt, P × P ; and Black wins a piece.

Trap No. 15 – Queen's Gambit Accepted. 1. P – Q4, P – Q4 ; 2. P – QB4, P × P ; 3. Kt – KB3, Kt – KB3 ; 4. P – K3, B – Kt5 ; 5. B × P, P – B4? (P – K3!) ; 6. B × P ch!, K × B ; 7. Kt – K5 ch, followed by 8. Kt × B. White has won a pawn and Black cannot castle.

Trap No. 16 – King's Indian Defence. 1. P – Q4, Kt – KB3 ; 2. P – QB4, P – KKt3 ; 3. P – KKt3, B – Kt2 ; 4. B – Kt2, Castles ; 5. Kt – KB3, P – Q3 ; 6. Castles, P – B4 ; 7. Kt – B3, Kt – B3 ; 8. P – Q5, Kt – QR4 ; 9. P – Kt3? (9. Kt – Q2 or 9. Q – Q3), Kt – K5! wins at least the exchange for Black – a typical trap utilising a fianchettoed bishop.

You will note that all except four of these traps occur in king's pawn openings, and that in the great majority of them White wins. This is no accident, and the moral is that if you are Black against 1. P – K4, you should look to the safety of your king and get castled as quickly as possible.

Chapter Nine

WHAT TO DO IN THE MIDDLE GAME

A GREAT MASTER, Richard Teichmann, once said that 'Chess is 95 per cent tactics'. And he was referring to the games of masters, who make a lifetime study of the game and whose chess is practically free from blunders. Even if you allow that Teichmann's statement is exaggerated, it still remains true that the decisive factor in the majority of master games is a tactical coup which one player saw and the other didn't. In master chess, the main tactical line quite often doesn't appear in the actual game because the loser avoids it and chooses a different and longer way of losing ; but in amateur games, the possibility of combinations, many of which are missed, occur all the time.

How do you know when a combination is possible ? It's easy enough, many people complain, to spot a combination when you are set a position in a chess magazine or book, because you know that there must be a surprise solution to 'White to play and win' ; but how can you afford the time to look at every possible move in your own games from this viewpoint ? The answer is that it is possible to recognise *patterns* of combinations which recur again and again ; once you know the way in which particular types of weakness can be generally exploited, you are more than half-way to recognising such combinational possibilities when they occur in your own games.

Most kinds of combinations or decisive coups revolve round one of two things : a *double attack* or an *insufficiently protected piece*. The double attack can be viewed in this way ; in chess, the players can only make one move at a time, so that if you can make a move which faces your opponent with two threats simultaneously, he will normally only be able to parry one of them. Of course this is particularly true when one of the attacked units is the king ; the king must escape from check, and then the second attack or threat to a piece succeeds automatically.

75

The second case, that of the insufficiently protected piece, is a mirror image of the double attack. If an attacked piece is guarded by one other piece, then an attack by the opponent on that second piece means that something must be lost.

What does this mean you should do in your own games? Before every move, take a look round the board to see if there are any attacks possible on unguarded or insufficiently protected pieces, and whether pieces can combine in attacks on some vital square, be it your own or your opponents. This sounds a long-winded process, and indeed it may be so when you first practice it ; but as you become accustomed to the types of combination which most commonly occur and find similar positions happening in your own games, you will find that the process of inspection of the board takes only a few seconds.

TYPES OF COMBINATION TO LOOK FOR

The Fork.
The fork is the simplest example in chess of the ' double attack ' type of combination. Any piece can fork ; even a king often attacks two men simultaneously in the later stages of a game. The hardest type of fork to see for the beginner is a knight fork, because of the strangeness and apparently ungeometrical character of the knight's move. To help you, here's a useful tip : place two chess pieces in at least thirty different situations in which a knight can fork them, and actually move the knight to make the fork. It may seem a futile exercise, but like practising scales in music, it saves you time later on. Then do the same with pawn forks, rook forks, bishop forks, and queen forks.

Even among experts, elementary forks can decide important games. The position in Figure 42 was decisive in winning the 1957 British Championship for Dr. Stephen Fazekas. His final move was 1. Q × R ch!, after which Black resigned, because after 1. ..., K × Q ; 2. Kt – K6 ch, followed by 3. Kt × Q, he is a whole rook down.

Figure 43 is more complicated. At first sight, White wins by the elementary knight fork 1. Kt × P, attacking both rooks, but then comes the reply 1. ..., Kt – Kt5! (threatening

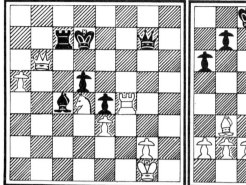
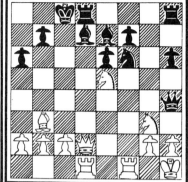

Fig. 42 – White to move and win.   *Fig. 43 – White to move and win.*

mate) ; 2. P – KR3, Q × Kt ; 3. P × Kt, Q – R5 ch ; 4. K – Kt1, B – B4 ch ; and it is White who is likely to lose the game. The moral is that when you make a combinative attack on an ordinary piece, look out for any chance of a counter-attack on a more valuable piece, especially if that piece be the king. This particular counter-attack with queen and knight against KR7 is considered later on in this chapter.

Nevertheless, there is a win based on a fork in Figure 43. White attacks the black QB with as many pieces as defend it, and in addition the rook at KR1, snug as it seems, depends for its protection on two pieces, the QR and the knight, which are also tied to the defence of this same QB. From this, the solution is a matter of logic : 1. Q – B3 ch, K – Kt1 ; 2. Kt × B ch, Kt × Kt ; 3. R × Kt, Resigns, for a piece is lost (Tal–Larsen, Portoroz 1958). Here the queen fork combined with the exploitation of the overload of Black's rook and knight, which were assigned to do too much – a double job in protection.

The Tie.

Figure 43 has already shown us something of a tie in operation. It occurs when a piece is used to defend something (a piece or a vital square) which is attacked, and then gets itself

77

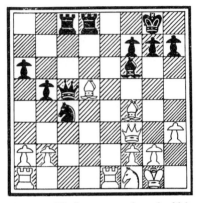

Fig. 44 – Black to move ; how should he capture the bishop ?

attacked from another direction ; this is what happens to the black knight and rook in Figure 43.

To avoid ties, protect attacked pieces with pawns or move them away when feasible in preference to protecting them with other pieces.

In Figure 44, Black should play 1. ..., R × B. Instead, he replied 1. ..., Q × B? immediately creating a tie : his rook at Q1 is now tied simultaneously to protecting the queen and guarding the back rank, and White wins by 2. R – K8 ch, R × R ; 3. Q × Q.

The Pin.
The pin is really another kind of fork, the difference being that the attack takes place all along one line (file, rank, or diagonal).

The commonest types of pin are those where a bishop or rook attacks a piece which is unable to move because of the exposure of a more important piece behind it. The most usual bishop pin occurs in some situation like : White B at KKt5, Kt at KB3, P at K4 ; Black Q at K2, Kt at KB3, Ps at KKt2, K3 (irrelevant pieces omitted). White to play wins a piece by 1. P – K5.

With the rook, the chief danger comes when the opposing king has stayed too long in the centre and gets into trouble on the king's file.

A typical example (irrelevant pieces omitted) is White R at K1, P at KB2 ; Black K at K1, Kt at K5, P at KB4. White to play wins a piece by 1. P – KB3.

In view of these dangers, one of the most glaring ways of asking for trouble is to leave the king and queen on the same diagonal as an enemy bishop, or the same file as an enemy rook. Even when there are several pieces in between the pinner and the threatened major pieces, ways to create a combination can often be found.

After White's initial mistake in Figure 45 of placing his king and queen on a diagonal which Black's QB can reach, the win is easy : 1. K – B1, R × B ; 2. R × R, R × R ; 3. Q × R, B – B5.

The Skewer.

The skewer is another type of danger to which a player is exposed who leaves pieces on the same file or diagonal.

In the pin, a minor piece cannot move because of exposing a major piece behind it ; in the skewer, a major piece is forced to move and so expose another piece behind it. In Figure 46 (in which Black, the victim, was no less a personage than a former world champion, Dr. Max Euwe !) White wins by 1. R × Kt, K × R ; 2. B – R4 ch.

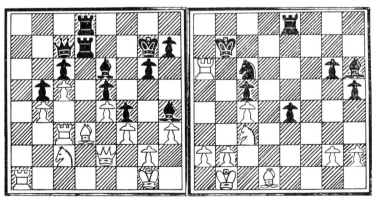

Fig. 45 – White plays 1. K – B1?   *Fig. 46 – White to move and win.*

The Net.

You should watch out for a 'net' when a piece has only one escape route from its actual square and can be threatened by an opposing piece of lesser value. The Noah's Ark Trap (p. 72) is one example of a net ; there the bishop is enveloped by the oncoming enemy pawns. Knights are also liable to be netted by pawns if they are left unsupported in the middle of the board. E.g. white pawns at KB3, KKt2, KR2 ; black knight at KKt4, pawns at K3, KB2, KKt2, KR2 (inessential pieces omitted) ; White to play wins a piece by P – KR4.

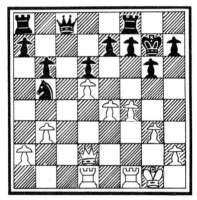

Fig. 47 – White to move and win.

In this position, won by world champion Mikhail Botvinnik of Russia, the net is combined with a fork : 1. R – B1, Q – Q2 (or 1. ..., Kt – B2 ; 2. Q – B3 ch) ; 2. P – QR4, and the knight is so far netted that it must retreat to where it can be forked : 2. ..., Kt – B2 ; 3. Q – B3 ch, or 2. ..., Kt – R6 ; 3. Q – Kt2 ch.

TYPES OF ATTACK ON THE KING

In one respect, the net is one of the most important of all types of combinative attacks, for any checkmate involves restriction or obstruction of the king's escape square and then a decisive threat – the same process as in a net. But attacks on the king generally fall into their own special, recognisable types. As in the case of the material-winning combinations which have been considered so far, if you remember the basic *patterns* of mating attacks, you will find that opportunities for them constantly crop up in your own games.

One checkmating attack into which almost all inexperienced players fall at least once is the threat to the back rank, occurring when none of the pawns in front of the king has been moved. A stock case is White : K at KKt1, R at K1, Ps at QR2, KKt2, KR3 ; Black : K at KKt1, R at QR1, Ps at KB2, KKt2, KR2. With Black to move, the beginner's blunder is 1. ..., R × P?? ; 2. R – K8 mate.

Even such an elementary combination can recur as high up as master chess in a more sophisticated form.

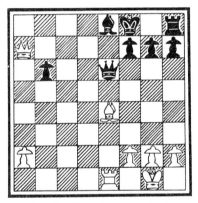

Fig. 48 – White to move and win.

Here (Evans–Bisguier, New York 1958–9), White wins by a combination of pin, double attack, and back rank mate : 1. Q – R3 ch, Q – K2 (if K – Kt1 ; 2. B × P ch, with a double attack on the king and queen) ; 2. B – B6!, Q × Q (the queen is pinned and cannot capture the rook) ; 3. R × B mate. Another very common type of attack on the king occurs where the KKtP has been advanced to KKt3, leaving 'holes' for the enemy pieces to invade at KR3 and KB3. The advance of the KKtP one square in front of the castled king is only good if the formation also contains a fianchettoed bishop at KKt2. Consequently, the other player often aims at the exchange of this bishop so as to facilitate the attack on the king.

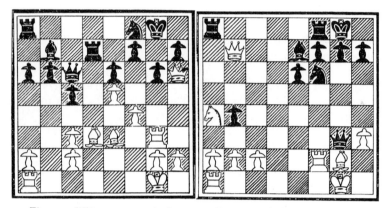

Fig. 49 – White to move and win. *Fig. 50 – Black to move and win.*

In Figure 49 (Olafsson–Pilnik, match 1957) is a typical mating attack against a king's position weakened by the advance of the KKtP. White wins by 1. P – B5 (threatening a 'net' of the black king by queen and pawn with 2. P – B6), P × P ; 2. B – KKt5, Kt – K3 (if 2. ..., P – B3 ; 3. B – B4 ch, K – R1 ; 4. B × P ch) ; 3. B – B6, P – KB5 (Black has defended against the immediate threat to his KKt2, but the fact that the white bishop also controls White's KR8 leads to another mating finish) ; 4. Q × RP ch!, K × Q ; 5. R – R3 ch, K – Kt1 ; 6. R – R8 mate.

Another type of attack which is very common is a combined attack against the square KR2 in front of the castled king. Very often KR2, like KKt2, is only guarded by the king and is therefore specially vulnerable to attack.

In Figure 50 (Darga–Portisch, Hastings 1958–9), Black wants to play 1. ..., B – Q3 so as to attack KR2 with his queen and bishop ; but if he plays it at once, White replies after 1. ..., B – Q3 ; with 2. Kt – Kt6, Q – R7 ch ; 3. K – B1, and the outcome is not clear. So Black plays 1. ..., Kt – Q4! (threatening ..., Kt – B5 ; followed by ..., Kt × P ch) ; and after 2. QR – KB1, B – Q3 ; White resigned, for if 3. R – K1, R × Kt wins a piece.

Queen and knight in combination against KR2 are also a striking force which you should bear in mind.

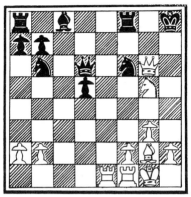

Fig. 51 – White to move and win.

In Figure 51 White's queen and knight are already converged for the attack, he must deflect Black's knight which is guarding the vital square. So 1. R – K8!, Kt × R (if R × R ; 2. Kt – B7 mate) ; 2 Q – R7 mate.

POSITIONAL PLAY

While you are still a beginner, you will find that opportunities to make combinations usually occur haphazardly, through simple oversights by you or your opponent. But as you progress beyond this stage, these opportunities usually need to be foreseen a move or so ahead, and in many positions there will be no tactical resource available at all. Many players find that the hardest part of chess to master is what to do when there is no obvious plan of attack, or when the opening is over and you are not sure what to do in the middle game. When you get to such a position, keep in mind these two rules :

1. Look around for any of your pieces which are not in play and whose position can be improved ; if you can see nothing more positive to do, simply move your *worst-posted* piece to a better position.

2. As a general aim of your strategy in positions where there is no combination possible and no likelihood of attacking the king, aim at tying down the enemy pieces to the defence of a fixed weakness in his position. A fixed weakness is a pawn that cannot safely move and cannot be defended by

another pawn, or a square in the centre or enemy camp which it is impossible for the enemy to defend with a pawn. Such squares are usually best occupied by your minor pieces. In the case of a weak pawn, the fact that your pieces are attacking it and your opponent's defending it will ensure that you have the initiative and (usually) control of the greater part of the board. Once you have the initiative, your chances of bringing off a combination or an attack on the king steadily increase.

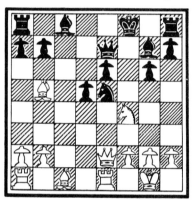

Fig. 52 – White to move ; how should he improve his position ?

Here (Penrose–Barden, London 1959) White has sacrificed a pawn for the attack : Black has a backward pawn at K3 and his queen and king are on the same diagonal, but there is no combination available yet. So White looks around for his worst placed piece ; this is the QR, with the QB a close second. White therefore plays 1. B – Q2 (better than B – K3, which would interfere with the pressure on the backward pawn), Q – R5 ; 2. QR – B1 (the rook belongs on an open file), P – QR3. And now, already, White can decide the game by a combination, although quite a complicated one : 3. R × B ch!, R × R ; 4. Kt × P ch, K – B2 ; 5. Kt × B, Kt – Kt5 ; 6. Q – K6 ch!, K × Kt ; 7. Q – Q7 ch, Resigns.

In Figure 53 (Nedeljkovic–Kieninger, Vienna 1957), Black's K3 cannot be defended by a pawn, and White occupies it by means of a little combination based on the pin of Black's

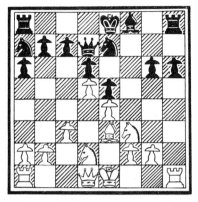

Fig. 53 – White, to move, can aim to occupy a fixed weak square.

KRP against his rook. 1. Kt – Kt5!, Kt – Kt1 (White threatened 2. Q – B3 as well) ; 2. Kt – K6, P – B4 ; 3. Kt – QB4, Kt – B1 ; 4. Q – B3, B – Kt2 ; 5. P – R4, P – Kt3 (not 5. ..., P – QKt4 ; 6. P × P, Q × P ; because of the fork 7. Kt – B7 ch) ; 6. Q – Kt4, K – B2 ; 7. P – B4 (the effect of White's occupation of the weak square has been to reduce all Black's pieces to passivity, so that White can now begin the decisive attack), P – QKt4 ; 8. RP × P, Q × P ; 9. Kt –

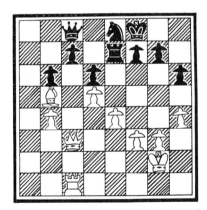

Fig. 54 – White, to move, wins because of Black's backward pawn.

B7! (the combination) and Black resigned, because if 9. ...,
Q × Kt ; 10. Q – K6 ch, K – B1 ; 11. Q – K8 mate.

Figure 54 (Flohr–Johner, Zurich 1934) is a typical example
of the evil consequences of a backward pawn. White wins by
1. Q – QB6 (threatening to exploit the pin on Black's queen
by 2. Q × KtP, P × Q ; 3. R × Q), P – B4 (a desperate
counter-attack) ; 2. R – R1!, and Black's position is so
cramped that he has no defence to 3. R – R8, winning either
the queen or a whole rook.

GENERAL ADVICE ON THE MIDDLE GAME

The *queen's* function in the middle game is that of a general ;
she should be kept as mobile as possible, ready to go to any
part of the board where an attack develops. Isolated raids
by the queen are usually as bad in the middle game as they
are in the opening. Use her in combination with the rooks
to support an attack on enemy backward pawns or in
controlling an open file ; in combination with the bishops in
long-range attacks on the enemy king (see Figures 49 and 50) ;
in similar combination with the knights ; and in supporting
a general advance of pawns on either flank.

The *rooks* should be able to find open files as the middle
game proceeds, and from there they can aim at entry to the
enemy position (e.g. Figure 52). If there are no open files,
you can usually create them by advancing pawns with the
rooks behind them.

The *bishops* are very strong on adjacent diagonals directed
against the opposing king. As pieces are exchanged and the
endgame approaches, it very often pays to switch the direction
of attack of your bishops to the queen's side, to support an
attack against the enemy pawns there. The bishops can also
often occupy weak squares in the centre and join from there
in supporting a king's side attack.

The *knights* should look for secure squares in the centre
(see Figure 53) from which they cannot be driven away by
enemy pawns. If your opponent has an isolated pawn (one
which cannot be supported by its own pawns) the square in
front of it usually makes an ideal knight outpost for you. If

you yourself have an isolated pawn, try and use the squares which the pawn guards as knight outposts.

The *pawns* must be handled with great care, for a bad pawn formation is a great handicap (see Figures 53 and 54). In particular, avoid the common mistake of leaving a lot of pawns on the same coloured squares as your bishop (when the other bishop has been exchanged). If you have both bishops left, aim to exchange off the one most handicapped by pawns and try to leave your opponent with such a bishop.

Positively, you can use a mobile mass of pawns in a storming advance on the enemy king (although make sure, if you have castled on the same side as your opponent, that your own king does not become too exposed as a result). If you have a QRP and QKtP on the queen's side against your opponent's QRP, QKtP, and QBP (a very common happening in queen's side openings such as the Queen's Gambit), you can advance your two pawns with a rook behind them ; when pawn exchanges eventually take place as a result, you can often arrange it that you have an open file for your rook and your opponent has a backward pawn.

Another quite common situation is a complete chain of pawns across the board ; say White pawns at QR2, QKt2, QB3, Q4, K5, KB4, KKt2, KR2 ; Black pawns at QR2, QKt4, QB5, Q4, K3, KB2, KKt3, KR2. Here you should aim to open files for your rooks by breaking through the base of your opponent's chain ; this means that White aims at P – KB5 and Black at P – QKt5.

Chapter Ten

THE PIECES IN THE ENDING

THE ENDGAME BEGINS when the forces are so reduced that mating attacks are unlikely to be successful with the pieces that remain. So when the king does not have to take extra precautions for its safety, it follows that it can and ought to be brought into an active part in the game. Usually, this means bringing it to the centre of the board, where it can be directed to either wing according to how the endgame develops.

The principle of the *activity* of the king is also applied to other pieces in the ending. The lazy workman slows up a job much more when there are only three people working than when there are six, and an inactive or useless piece is a greater handicap in the ending than at any other time.

So the first and basic rule in the ending, even before thinking of passed pawns, is : *Get your pieces into aggressive positions.*

Generally, ideal positions for each piece are :

QUEEN – in the centre of the board.

ROOK – On an open file, and if possible on the seventh rank where it can harass the enemy pawns and hem in the enemy king. An aggressive position for the rook becomes more and more essential the fewer pieces are on the board. If there are still several minor pieces (knights and bishops) left, you need to take care lest a premature invasion of the seventh by your rook leads to it being trapped by the minor pieces. Remember, a rook has only one retreat road.

BISHOP – Where it controls one of the two central diagonals. This does not necessarily mean that the bishop needs to be posted on a central square ; a fianchettoed bishop on KKt2 can exert considerable pressure both on the centre and against the opposing queen's side pawns.

KNIGHT – On a square in the centre of the board or near to

the enemy position ; supported by one of its own pawns and not vulnerable to attack by an enemy pawn.

KING – At or near the centre. The king, besides being ready to invade the enemy camp and join in an attack on his pawns, may also serve a defensive role in guarding groups of his own pawns from attack by the opposing knights and bishops ; he can also often prevent an invasion of an enemy rook to the seventh or eighth ranks.

As an illustration of how an endgame may be decided just because one player's pieces are more active than his opponent's men, here is a position from the 1958 British Championship.

Fig. 55 – Black should keep his rook active.

Here Black made an instructive mistake ; he could have drawn fairly easily by 1. ..., R – Q7 ; 2. R × P, K – K2 ; 3. P – QKt4, R – Kt7 ; when although he is a pawn down, his rook and king are *active* and White's *passive*.

Instead, Black continued 1. ..., R – Kt2? ; 2. K – K2, K – K2 ; 3. K – Q3, K – Q3 ; 4. K – Q4, P – B3 ; 5. P – QKt4, P – Kt3 ; 6. P – Kt4, R – Kt1 (this is what happens when an endgame position becomes too passive ; Black can do nothing but mark time) ; 7. P – R4, R – Kt2 ; 8. P – B3, R – Kt1 ; 9. P – R5, P × P ; 10. R × RP, R – Kt2 ; 11. R – KB5, K – K3 ; and now came the invasion by the white king : 12. K – B5, R – Kt1 ; 13. K – B6, R – B1 ch ;

14. K × P. White has now converted his positional advantage into a winning material one. The remaining moves are also instructive. 14. ..., R – B6 ; 15. K – Kt6, P – R4 ; 16. R × P, R × P ; 17. P – QKt5, R – KKt6 ; 18. R – R4, K – Q3 ; 19. K – Kt7, R – Kt6 ; 20. P – Kt6, R – Kt5 ; 21. R – R6, R × P ; 22. R × P ch, K – Q2 ; 23. R – B7 ch, K – Q3 ; 24. R – B7, R – Kt8 ; 25. R – B2. This position is also a very instructive one, and deserves a diagram.

Fig. 56 – Winning a rook ending a pawn up.

In any rook and pawn ending in which one side is a pawn up, the win can be forced if the stronger side's king is on the sixth rank in front of the pawn and the enemy king is cut off from the file on which the pawn stands. The only exception to this is the RP, which as we saw in Chapter 5, often creates special problems.

The final moves were 25. ..., R – Kt8 ; 26. K – R7, K – Q2 ; 27. P – Kt7, R – R8 ch ; 28. K – Kt8, R – QKt8 ; 29. R – QR2, R – Kt6 ; 30. K – R8, K – B2 ; 31. R – B2 ch, Resigns.

The second rule to follow in all endgames is : *Aim to create a passed pawn.* A passed pawn will usually tie down at least one of the enemy pieces to watching it or blockading it, and this means that your other pieces will have increased scope in other parts of the board. A passed pawn which is left free to advance may become the means of a winning

combination to force it through to queen, and this also applies
to any pawn which is far up the board.

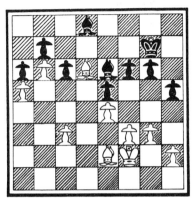

*Fig. 57 – Black to move ; what is the
threat ?*

In Figure 57 (Barden–Phillips, London 1958), Black, in
time trouble, played 1. ..., K – B2? (1. ..., B – B1 is necessary)
and was surprised by the reply 2. B × RP!, for if 2. ..., P × B ;
3. P – Kt7, and the pawn queens.

Now a rule which is important whether you are attacking
or defending in an endgame : *when you are trying to win, keep
pawns on both sides of the board if possible.* The reason for this
is that it gives you, assuming you have the initiative or an
extra pawn, a chance of tying your opponent down on the
wing where you are stronger and then making a decisive
penetration on the opposite side. Conversely, if you are on
the defensive, try to eliminate all the pawns on one wing.
When there are pawns left on only one side of the board, an
extra pawn is much less likely to win.

Rules for exploiting a material advantage.

If you are a pawn or pawns ahead in an ending, *exchange
pieces* (not pawns) whenever this can be done without losing
ground positionally. This is a rule which holds with only
two main exceptions. One is when exchanges of pieces leave
you with a bishop operating on one colour square against

your opponent's bishop working on the other. A second danger is that you will reach a position in which you have bishop and knight or two knights against two bishops. Two bishops, which can attack on both wings, are specially useful in the ending, unless the pawn position is very blocked. Another danger of having bishop and knight against two bishops is that the knight is restricted in scope by having to avoid squares on which it can be exchanged so as to leave a bishops of opposite colour ending.

Easiest Endings to Win.

King and pawn endings with a pawn ahead are the easiest of all to win, *unless* the weaker side's king is decidedly better placed than the stronger's. A typical instance would be when one side is a pawn behind, but has his king on the fourth rank against his opponent's on the third, and also has the opposition.

Next to king and pawn endings, knight and pawn endings are the easiest to win with a pawn up (except where there is only one pawn, when the weaker side's knight can usually be sacrificed).

Remember this point – many club players, fearing the powers of a knight, mistakenly think that knight endings must be very difficult.

Bishop endings (except, as already mentioned, where the bishops are on opposite coloured squares) are also comparatively easy, with the proviso that you should beware of putting your pawns on the same coloured squares as your own bishop, unless it is reasonably certain that they will be able to advance further. Every one of your pawns on the same coloured square as your bishop decreases its scope ; in fact, many endings are won without material advantage because one side has a ' good ' bishop unhindered by its own pawns and the other player has a ' bad ' bishop with very little scope at all.

Another ending of the same type is where one side has a bishop handicapped by its own pawns and the other has a knight. In such cases, the player with the knight can usually infiltrate with his king along the squares of the colour which the bishop does not control. Very different is the case where the bishop is not restricted by its own pawns. Then the bishop's power of long-range movement, compared with the short-stepping knight, is worth practically the equivalent of a full pawn.

Queen and pawn endings with a pawn ahead are usually won if the extra pawn is passed, although the winning process is normally very laborious because of the care needed to avoid perpetual check by the opposing queen.

The type of ending which gives most chances to the defending side is rook and pawn endings. Here an aggressive rook position often makes up for, or even outweighs, the disadvantage of being a pawn down. This is the vital factor to remember in all rook endings ; and from the fact that the rook should be used actively, it follows that it is best placed behind and not in front of a passed pawn. This statement, however, needs some qualification. If the passed pawn (whether it be yours or your opponent's) is still far back, on the second or third rank, you may find in some cases that your rook exerts greater control over the board by being placed in front of the pawn.

But if the passed pawn is on the fourth rank or further, *always put your rook behind it if possible.* If the rook is behind your own passed pawn, you will find that the rook's scope is steadily enhanced as the pawn advances up the board ;

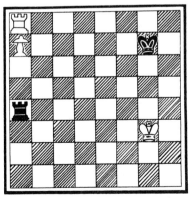

Fig. 58 – How does Black draw ?

while if your rook is behind a passed pawn of your opponent's, he will usually be obliged to protect it with his own rook from the side or front, and his rook will then be tied to the few squares from which it can protect the pawn.

One tactical device must be watched out for in a rook and pawn ending in which a passed pawn is far advanced.

In Figure 58 Black can draw by 1. ..., K – R2 ; followed by shuttling the king between R2 and Kt2. White can advance his king up the board as far as QKt6, but when he gets there Black can arrange to have his rook on QR8 and then check the king from behind *ad infinitum*. *But* if Black is so incautious as to play 1. ..., K – B2? White wins by 2. R – R8, R × P ; 3. R – R7 ch, the skewer combination in action in the end-game.

Don't try to remember all the general remarks in this chapter at the first reading ; rather you should turn back to them whenever you have played an ending in your own games, and try to work out just where you went wrong – if you did !

Chapter Eleven

A COMPLETE GAME ANALYSED

YOU CAN PLAY over master games for one or both of two reasons ; to improve your own standard and simply to enjoy them. But if you do want to improve at chess, you shouldn't play over games casually, without thinking about the moves. The best idea is to cover up the moves made by the winner and work them out for yourself ; in this way it will be like playing your own game and getting coaching from an expert who shows you what you should have done.

Here is a game from the last international congress at Hastings. These congresses are held every year immediately after Christmas and, besides the international event to which the greatest masters from all over the world are invited, there are subsidiary tournaments for every class of player. One excellent way of taking an intellectual holiday and at the same time improving your game is to compete in one of these congresses. Besides Hastings, there are congresses at Bognor, Richmond, Southend, and Salford at Easter, at Ilford and Scunthorpe at Whitsun, an annual event organised by the magazine *Chess*, usually at Whitby in September, and the British Chess Federation's annual congress, which incorporates the British Men's and Ladies' Championships, held in a different town each year in the second half of August.

The winner of this game, Wolfgang Uhlmann, a young accountant from East Germany, is one of the best of the many fine players who have come to the front in Eastern Europe since the war. His opponent is Bob Wade, a New Zealander who has resided in England for several years and who won the British Championship in 1952. The present game is by no means representative of his normal style, for usually he is one of the toughest and most determined of masters ; but even the best players have their off-days.

White	*Black*
(Wolfgang Uhlmann)	(Bob Wade)

Hastings, 1958–9

Queen's Gambit Accepted

1. P – Q4	P – Q4
2. P – QB4	P × P

The Queen's Gambit is one which many players prefer to decline by 2. ..., P – K3 or 2. ..., P – QB3, since the acceptance of the gambit requires very precise play on Black's part. To decline it, as many players do, by 2. ..., Kt – KB3, allows White to obtain an advantage in the centre very quickly by 3. P × P, Kt × P (3. ..., Q × P ; 4. Kt – QB3, Q – Q1 ; 5. P – K4 is even worse) ; 4. Kt – KB3 (better than 4. P – K4 at once), Kt – QB3 ; 5. P – K4, Kt – B3 ; 5. P – Q5, Kt – QKt1 ; 6. Kt – B3, and the superiority of White's position is obvious.

3. Kt – KB3

3. P – K4 looks the obvious move, to get two pawns abreast in the centre, but this is answered by 3. ..., P – QB4 ; 4. P – Q5, P – K3 ; 5. B × P (if 5. P × P, Q × Q ch ; 6. K × Q, B × P and White does not even get his pawn back), P × P ; 6. B × P (if 6. P × P, B – Q3 and Black completes his development without trouble), B – Q3 (not, however, 6. ..., Kt – KB3 ; 7. B × P ch!, and if 7. ..., K × B ; 8. Q × Q, a common tactical trap to watch for whenever there is a bishop bearing on KB7) ; 7. Kt – KB3, Kt – KB3 ; 8. P – K5, Kt × B ; 9. Q × Kt, B – K2 ; and Black, having survived White's attack, can safely complete his development and then start the middle game with the advantage of the two bishops.

3. ...   P – QB4

3. ..., Kt – KB3 (developing a piece) is the usual and rather preferable move here. Many inexperienced players try to hang on to the gambit pawn by 3. ..., P – QKt4 ; but this leads to great difficulties after 4. P – K3, P – QR3 ; 5. P – QR4, P – QB3 ; 6. Kt – K5, e.g. 6. ..., P – K3 ; 7.

Q – B3, Kt – B3 ; 8. P × P, and Black cannot recapture either way because of the pin on his rook.

4. P – Q5	Kt – KB3?

This is now a serious tactical mistake ; Black, as we shall see, ought to have played 4. ..., P – K3 now, and if 5. Kt – B3, P × P ; 6. Kt × P, Kt – KB3.

5. Kt – B3	P – K3

Black wants to attack White's pawn and at the same time develop his KB. 5. ..., B – B4 looks more obvious as a developing move, but then comes 6. Kt – KR4, B – Kt3 ; 7. Kt × B, RP × Kt ; 8. P – K4, and White has the two bishops and a strong centre. Any other move, like 5. ..., QKt – Q2 merely allows White to consolidate his hold on the board by 6. P – K4, followed by B × P. To permit your opponent such a terrific centre is, at master level, practically equivalent to loss of the game ; hence Black must counter-attack, whatever the cost.

6. P – K4	P × P

Now Black expects 7. P × P, when he can follow up by 7. ..., B – Q3 ; 8. B × P, Castles ; with a satisfactory game. A blocked, isolated pawn in the centre is generally inferior to an opponent's mobile majority of pawns on a wing.

7. P – K5

A shock to Black ; now if he replies 7. ..., Kt – K5 ; 8. Kt × P, B – K3 ; 9. B × P, White clearly has the advantage with a supported knight outpost in the centre, whereas Black's own advanced knight is too isolated to be effective.

7. ...	P – Q5
8. B × P	

White could also play 8. P × Kt, P × Kt ; 9. Q × Q ch, K × Q ; 10. B – Kt5.

8. ...	Kt – B3?

This is immediately fatal. His only hope was 8. ..., P × Kt ; 9. B × P ch (remember this typical tactic when the queens are facing each other and one is only protected by its king), K – K2 ; 10. P × Kt ch, P × P ; 11. Q – Kt3, P × P ; 12. B × P, although then Black's chances of survival, with his king permanently trapped in the centre, are slight. The important point for beginners to note is the hopeless position of a player whose king cannot castle when the centre files are open.

| 9. P × Kt | P × Kt |
| 10. Q – K2 ch! | |

Black had not anticipated this ; now he must either allow his king to be driven into the open or else lose a piece after 10. ..., B – K3 ; 11. B × B, P × B ; 12. Q × P ch, forcing 12. ..., B – K2 ; 13. P × B.

| 10. ... | K – Q2 |

Some of you may think that master chess is always a matter of deadly earnestness, but at this point both players wore broad smiles, and one of the expert spectators jokingly asked Wade if his king liked being a tourist.

11. B – B4

Simple and strong. If you have a good position with no counter-chances for your opponent but do not see an immediate way of winning, a sound and simple policy is to look for a move which improves your control of the board or strengthens your position still further.

| 11. ... | Q – R4 |

White threatened, among other things, 12. R – Q1 ch, Kt – Q5 ; 12. Kt × Kt, winning at least a piece. Now Black sets a desperate trap : if 12. R – Q1 ch, Kt – Q5 ; 13. Kt × Kt, P – B7 dis. ch and Black may even win (14. R – Q2, P – B8 (Q) ch).

| 12. R – Q1 ch | Kt – Q5 |
| 13. B – Kt5 ch! | |

A type of move which is obvious once it is played, but which many would not see until it was pointed out to them. Since the pinned knight on Black's Q5 cannot move, his double protection of his QKt4 is illusory.

13. ...   Q × B

The choice lies between this move, 13. ..., K – Q1 ; 14. Q – K8 mate, and resignation. The last is the most appropriate, but Black sets a final trap.

14. Q × Q ch   K – K3.

Now, Black's knight is no longer pinned and threatens to capture the queen.

15. Kt × Kt ch   P × Kt
16. R × P   Resigns

Black's king is his only developed piece !

Chapter Twelve

WHERE DO YOU GO FROM HERE?

SOME READERS WILL only have read this book so as to play occasional games with their friends ; others will have become interested enough to want to advance further, and it is for this group that this last chapter is written.

If you have little time to devote to chess, then to practice against opponents of your own strength is one of the less helpful methods of improving. You will do better by playing over games from newspapers and magazines, covering up the winner's moves and working them out for yourself. The best games to study are those in which there is an annotated commentary to the play, so that when your move differs from the one actually chosen you can find out the reason. Don't be discouraged if you find that you hardly ever hit on the same move as the master playing the game ; after all, he is an expert who has devoted much of his life to ensuring that he makes the best move. If you get a quarter of the moves right in a game, you are doing quite well. After you have been playing games over in this way for some weeks, you will find that you start to get more and more of the moves right, and this improvement will continue.

Another sound way of improving is to play chess by post. There are two large organisations (British Correspondence Chess Association, ' Ommaroo ', Hamesmoor Way, Mytchett, Aldershot, Hants, and the Postal Chess Club, Masonic Buildings, Sutton Coldfield, Warwickshire) which cater for postal players, and each has over a thousand members of all strengths from beginners upwards. In postal chess, the moves are sent in chess notation on chess score sheets from one opponent to the other ; the advantage of it is that, with almost unlimited time to analyse each move, even a comparative beginner can enjoy the satisfaction of playing a game with a logical pattern to it. One of the greatest living masters, Paul Keres of Russia, built up his chess strength by taking part in as many as 150 games by post simultaneously.

You should certainly invest in a few books, apart from this one. Reinfeld's *Chess for Amateurs* is a useful aid to the beginner ; it gives a series of games in which players make elementary and instructive mistakes and gives excellent advice on how to avoid them in your own play. At a more advanced level, there is the same author's *Chess Mastery by Question and Answer*, and my own book *How Good Is Your Chess ?* gives a selection of games in which the reader guesses each move and is awarded marks on the results to enable him to rate his own chess strength.

Now for more specialised books. In the openings, you should concentrate on the principles involved rather than on trying to learn variations off by heart. Golombek's *Modern Opening Chess Strategy* and my own *A Guide to Chess Openings* concentrate on these aspects. The best book for advice on the middle game is Euwe's *Judgment and Planning in Chess*, but an even more helpful way of studying chess strategy is to buy a book containing the games of a great master. The two most suitable to an inexperienced player, because of their detailed notes and clear explanations, are Botvinnik's *100 Selected Games* and Golombek's *Capablanca's 100 Best Games of Chess*. In the endgame, Euwe and Hooper's *A Guide to Chess Endings*, is most helpful both in explanation and as a reference work.

It is a good thing to join a chess club, if you have a flourishing one locally. A note of warning here : many chess clubs are completely unimaginative in providing such facilities as coffee, sandwiches, extra events in addition to ordinary club nights, and matches for the weaker members. So if your local club, on inspection, turns out to be moribund, consult your local library to see if there is another, more active one in the area. Many localities have several chess clubs.

Two particularly valuable methods of improving your play may not be open to everyone because of lack of time or inclination ; but if you can manage it, it is a good idea to find, persuade, or bribe a strong player who is willing to go over your games with you. He should be able to point out the types of mistake you are making, which is already half way to overcoming them. A second method which should help is to go to a chess tournament or match and watch the experts in action, again using the system of working out the likely move for yourself.

You can keep in touch with chess activities in this country by subscribing to one of the two chess magazines, *Chess* (obtainable from Masonic Buildings, Sutton Coldfield, Warwickshire ; issued fortnightly or monthly) and the *British Chess Magazine* (obtainable from 20 Cestnut Road, London S.E. 27 ; issued monthly). Finally, you may want to enter for one of the numerous annual chess congresses, which take place all over the country. The biggest are at Hastings over the New Year and at Bognor immediately after Easter. The British Chess Federation runs its own annual congress in August, and this includes the British Championship, for which anyone can enter on payment of a fee of 5s. The preliminary stages of the British Championship consist of a country-wide eliminating competition in which entrants are paired, initially with others from their own county, and then with those from neighbouring counties. The eliminating competitions bring the number of entrants down to 32, and these players meet in an eleven-round tournament during the annual congress. From the British Championship, the way is open to eliminating contests for the world title – but chess doesn't have to be taken that seriously. Even if you only play with friends or family and only once a year at Christmas, chess will repay you in pleasure for the time which you give to it.